Dog Rescue
A to Z

A Beginner's memoir

Books by Mary Blocksma

Adult Nonfiction
Dog Rescue A to Z: A Beginner's Memoir
Great Lakes Nature: An Outdoor Year
Lake Lover's Year: A Writer Learns to Paint
The Fourth Coast: Exploring the Great Lakes
Reading the Numbers: A Survival Guide
36 Years and 21 Homes, coauthor Ruth Blocksma

Children's Books
What's in the Woods?
What's On the Beach?
Ticket to the Twenties
Yoo Hoo, Moon!
Amazing Mouths and Menus
The Marvelous Music Machine

By Mary Blocksma & Dewey Blocksma
Action Contraptions
Easy-to-Make Water Toys That Really Work
Space-Crafting
Easy-to-Make Spaceships That Really Fly

Just One More Books:
All My Toys Are On the Floor
Where's That Duck?
What's in the Tub?
The Best Dressed Bear
Apple Tree! Apple Tree!
Grandma Dragon's Birthday
The Pup Went Up
Did You Hear That?

For all the good people
who rescue abandoned dogs
and those who support their efforts.

Hey, it's Shawna Guiett from
Amazing Grace Animal Rescue!
Good to see you again, Shawna!

Dog Rescue A to Z
A BEGINNER'S MEMOIR

Everything I learned from scratch
when I adopted Gracie

Mary Blocksma

Published by
Beaver Island Arts
BeaverIslandArts.com
mblocksma@yahoo.com
989-894-5925

Photograghs and drawings
are by Mary Blocksma.

The Gracie portrait by Jenny Blair
is used with permission.

ISBN 978-0-9708575-5-2

Printed by Holland Litho
Zeeland, Michigan USA

First Edition, 2015
10 9 8 7 6 5 4 3 2 1

Table of Contents

Dog Fever

When I adopted Gracie, I didn't know how much I didn't know, and no one was more surprised than I was—although everyone who knew me was really, really surprised—that I suddenly had a dog. Had I lost my mind? wondered my family and most of my friends. What had happened to my free spirit? I worried, too—how could I dream of going to Paris now?

A review of my typical coping behavior might explain it: Every time a serious relationship ends, I dream up a delightful, year-long project to distract me. It never starts out as a book, but writing books is what I do.

For example, after my second divorce, I decided to take four or five walks a week for a year, each time identifying some living thing. This became *Naming Nature,* re-issued as *Great Lakes Nature.* Years later, discovering my honey was secretly married, I rented a lakeside cottage and painted the view out the same window 160 times, watercolors later journaled in *Lake Lover's*

Year: A Writer Learns to Paint. So I should have expected that, after a recent break-up, my inner child would do something rash and demand a dog. She insisted. She even Googled rescue sites on the sly, pointing out this and that really nice dog.

I've learned to pay attention to that child, who knows my heart better than I do, so, over Christmas, I began looking at dogs online. Between *PetFinder.com* and *Adoptapet.com*, 3,467 dogs were available from more than fifty agencies, all within an hour's drive. If I'd known what I was looking for, I could have narrowed my search by breed, size, age and/or location. Lacking this knowledge, I clicked on one adorable dog photo after another. Some listings offered little information, while others resembled an online dating service.

Despite the variety, I couldn't relate to any particular dog, so I continued my search in person, depending on my insistent intuition to choose for me. I began with my local Bay City animal control shelter, where twenty big dogs, mostly pit bulls, barked in unison in metal-fenced pens. Overwhelmed, I returned to my computer and found a friendly-looking, medium-sized boxer at Amazing Grace Animal Rescue, half an hour away in Saginaw. I e-mailed the contact who quickly replied. The next day, on my way to see the boxer, I found Amazing Grace Animal Rescue in a nondescript, industrial district building.

I was welcomed into a large room by Shawna Guiett, a pleasant, white-haired woman, whom I had met online. A blanket-covered sofa and a kitchen table with two chairs furnished the stark gray area. Six large cats lounged about as a little dog scampered around us, woofed briefly and sprang to the sofa.

In a back room, large dogs barked and leapt upon their chain link enclosures. The boxer that had caught my eye online slowly rose as we entered his pen.

"He looks so sad," I said.

"Someone threw him out of a moving car," explained my guide. "He was observed and brought straight here."

I felt sorry for the boxer, but he seemed so big. We returned to the large room, sat on the sofa and the small dog jumped in my lap. I hadn't clicked on any small dog photos—I've never liked little yappy dogs—but this dog remained quiet despite the back-room din. Between brief periods on my lap, she propelled her tank-like body around the room on slender legs.

Shawna called her a Miniature Pinscher. I was put off by the breed name, but was quickly assured that, although a Min Pin resembles a Doberman, it's actually a terrier. Hating to vacuum, I noted her short-haired coat. Her age worked, too—she was four, which to me meant that she was over any annoying puppyness, but still had plenty of time left. And she was already spayed, now required by most shelters, and up-to-date on her shots. I paid the adoption fee ($75), signed some papers, and, practically before I knew it myself, I was heading home with my new pet.

I so disliked the saccharine name she came with, a new name was imperative, but what? My friends and even I expected something literary, like T.S. Eliot's cat names, which made it to Broadway. When I had cats, however, I always gave them buddy names like Charlie, Sam, or Maxie. In the end, I called my Min Pin Amazing Gracie, after the place where we'd met. She quickly began responding to her new name. Gracie is not an unusual pet name—so far we have met eight Gracies, canine and feline. However, my name is Mary and there are millions of us. Already, we had something in common.

Unfamiliarity with Min Pins was just the beginning of my doggie ignorance. The extent and pace of what I had to learn about Gracie, dogs in general and myself led me to log my almost daily lessons, arranged here in alphabetical categories. Our stories may be specific to a four-to-six-year-old fifteen-pound Min Pin living with a seventy-something weight-with-held woman, but most dog owners, especially new rescuers, will find themselves in these pages.

This is a memoir, not an expert guide: What follows describes the journey of new companions toward compatibility: successes, failures, training, indulgences, web sites, equipment, treats, toys, good advice and bad.

This is the book I wish I'd had when I adopted Gracie.

Abandonment

Most shelter dog backgrounds are unknown, but I did learn that Gracie's previous owner had gone to live with her mother, leaving both her dog and an abusive boyfriend. No shelter dog is quite like another, but they are all abandoned, unclaimed, or rescued, often from horrible circumstances. This may explain why most of these agencies insist that we provide a "furever home" for a would-be pet, something firmly impressed upon me: Following our two-week trial period, I had to pretty much promise to keep Gracie 'til death do us part. Obviously, no one can guarantee such a thing, life being unpredictable, but the rescue and animal control agencies, which frequently deal with the victims of sad circumstances and cavalier attitudes, do what they can to send their charges to a more secure future.

Understandably, many rescue and animal control agencies have all their cats and dogs spayed (females) or neutered (males) before allowing them to be adopted, adding the expense to the adoption fee. Sometimes this is part of the adoption agreement. I needed only glance at the extraordinary number of animal adoption agencies listed online, most of which were working at capacity, to ensure that no pet in my care adds to that number.

However, even as I recognized the good-hearted intention of calling a pet adoption a "furever home," there were times in my life when I had to part with a pet. I did not give up

I am so confused. What's going on here? Who is this person?

my Peace Corps calling for my cat, for which I found a loving home. I rehomed our collies when, forty years ago, my husband and I parted ways—working full time and caring for a young child, I was barely hanging on to sanity. Sometimes there's no point in everyone being miserable.

However, a situation that feels impossible may just need time. I did consider returning Gracie to the shelter after our stressful first Florida camping trip, but, as it turned out, we just needed a longer adjustment period. At the time, I was unaware how lucky I was to find Gracie. I later discovered that small dogs are often in demand, and Gracie had been at the shelter for less than a week.

Abuse

I decided on a rescue dog because I didn't want to train a puppy, and the potentially good deed helped me rationalize my desire to adopt a dog. I did worry that a shelter dog would come with baggage, which did hold true for Gracie. At first, Gracie trembled at every sound, small things at which today she'd not even prick up her ears. She shook so often and so hard that I worried my newly adopted pet was living in a constant state of fear, or at least on high alert as everything in her life was changing.

Gracie would not enter a bathroom or the basement, although she followed me everywhere else. She shrank from hands reaching to pet her, even from mine. She did not like

14

men, especially large men, snarling and barking incessantly at an imposing male visitor who, highly annoyed at this rejection, offered to buy me a "proper dog." (The two later developed a reluctant affection.)

After things settled down, and even adventure became routine, Gracie's occasional trembling seemed more inspired by the sight of an unusual dog or the prospect of a juicy hunk of meat. Or perhaps she'd just been outside on a chilly day. Time and repetition seem to have reassured her that harm is not lurking around every corner.

However, she can still be cautious with people she doesn't know. I suggest to strangers that they offer her the back of a hand to sniff before they pet her. I don't encourage children to pet Gracie, although often they ask. Gracie has never been unfriendly to children, but she still does freak out at fast-moving objects, animate and otherwise; I worry she might nip at an excited child. I recommend that children learn to use caution around dogs they don't know.

Trust between Gracie and me has taken time and testing, but, as it has grown, both our stress levels have diminished. At first, when I had no idea what I could trust Gracie to do, or not to do, I constantly worried and watched her. Before long, however, I relaxed, trusting her to respect my house, my belongings and my car. It may have taken Gracie a bit longer to believe that I'd never hit her, shut her up in a room by herself, or allow anyone to abuse her. Routine, repetition, consistency and dependable kindness seem to be working.

Adventure

Less than two weeks after I'd adopted Gracie, I packed up my 25-year-old, 19-foot Ford RV, and we left Michigan for sunny Florida. Although I'd checked the route weather online, either I or the forecasters were sorely mistaken. The previous year my RV trip south had been under clear and warming skies, but this year, it rained so hard I often had to pull off the highway. The van sprang leaks over the stove and the side door.

Gracie hated the rain. Apparently, one of the worst things that could happen to her was getting wet (an aversion that served for disciplinary purposes later.) Still, despite our few dry pit stops, she never soiled the RV. She gave me no clear signal when she had to go, so, still uncertain about her needs, I stopped every two hours instead of my usual four, each time looking for a gas station with a satisfactory patch of grass. We also frequented rest areas offering specified dog walks.

Gracie quickly learned that the driver was off-limits. When she wasn't curled up in the passenger seat or planting her nose on the passenger-side window to watch her new world roll by, she perched on the towel-covered plastic table I'd wedged between the front seats. Days, she had the run of the van. Nights, she burrowed under the blankets next to me.

This was the first time I'd allowed Gracie in my bed, and was she welcome! Night temperatures slipped into the thirties, but Gracie's body temperature, noticeably higher than my own, made meaningful the expression "two-dog night"—it would be a cold night indeed during which one Min Pin was not enough to keep me warm. The normal body temperature for a healthy dog, I learned later, ranges from 99 to 102.5 degrees, not impressively higher than my own 98.6, but those few degrees were gratefully felt.

At a Kentucky truck stop, someone forced opened the outside refrigerator access door, probably while I was in a Denny's eating a late dinner. I didn't notice the damaged door until the next morning on the road, when it flapped noisily. If it came off, I'd be in real trouble, exposing the backside of the refrigerator to the elements and the inside of the van to chilly drafts. After two unsuccessful attempts to fix it, I drove into a rest area, reached up and banged on one of the high semi-truck doors, and asked the driver if he could help. In minutes, he'd tied that door down with a piece of his own rope, and it stayed that way until two years later a friend fixed the latch.

In spite of everything—the pouring rain, the van damage, the stops along Interstate 65—and although we were still nervous and unsure of ourselves and each other, Gracie and I were both enjoying the road. This was a relief to me, as I am a life-long cross-country driver. I love that I can take off at a moment's notice and drive thousands of miles without a visa or anyone's permission, crossing state lines as if they didn't exist.

I was twenty-one when I set out on my first solo road trip—from Johns Hopkins in Baltimore, Maryland, to Grand Rapids, Michigan—and I've been an avid cross-country driver ever since. Driving is cheaper and more interesting than flying, I can stop where I like, or not, and I don't have to cram my life in a suitcase. Having lived in Colorado and California, I've practically worn tracks on Interstate 80, visiting family in Grand Rapids. During my twenty years back in Michigan, I've explored all the main routes to Florida. So I was glad to have a companion who loved the road.

I love visiting Florida, not just for the weather, but for the many friends and favorite cousins who, in the past, have invited me to visit. Touring them, I can go from Jacksonville to Cocoa Beach to Fort Lauderdale to Venice to Sarasota to Ocala, ending up in Cedar Key at an RV park, full of palm trees, seascapes and birds.

I love going to Shell Mound, near Cedar Key, Florida.
I hope no one trips on my line!

This year, not all went well. I had to say goodbye to some of my beloved destinations because our pets did not get along—someone's dog would not let Gracie on her territory, or Gracie would chase someone else's cats. However, when we got to Old Pear Tree Farm in Ocala, intending to visit my college friend Rowland Bennett and his wife Linda, we found ourselves at

That Gypsy! She thinks she's the boss
of Old Pear Tree Farm. She doesn't scare me, much.

home with animal lovers. Our hosts, Rowland's sister Pam Johnson and her husband Jim, gave Gracie and me a warm welcome, Pam providing some much-needed training. Populated by the Johnson's two dogs, two cats and twenty-five horses and ponies, plus five dogs who visited almost daily, the farm was a great place to learn how to live with dogs.

I often travel along the Gulf coast on my way home from Florida, keeping an eye on the weather, poised to shoot up Interstate 65 when things look clear. This year I was really eager

Free at last! I spent three days in that crazy crate!

to introduce Gracie to the gorgeous St. George Island State Park beaches, located at the end of a very long, thin peninsula. Despite our campsite reservations, however, we got no farther than the gate. Dogs, I was sternly warned, had to stay in the campground; no dogs were allowed on the beaches or the pavilions. A no-dogs-on-the-beach policy hadn't occurred to me, but I soon ran into it again at our next stop—Mexico Beach, another of my favorite Gulf coast camping spots. There, however, the RV park was pet-friendly, supplying poopy bags at a dog relief station. A sidewalk, from which I could enjoy the seaside while I walked the dog, ran along the beach.

It makes sense to keep feces out of the sand—I just hadn't thought of it. Now I've learned to ask about pet policies before making reservations. At least in Florida, it's not uncommon for dogs to be banned from beaches—in Fort Lauderdale, dogs aren't even allowed on the sidewalks that line them.

The second year I took Gracie to Florida, having been chastised by a dog trainer for allowing my dog to ride in glorious freedom, I seat-belted a metal crate into the passenger seat of my van. Gracie had been crate-trained and did not resist when I popped her in. She had room to stand up, turn around and lie down, but twelve hours a day for three days (and, two months later, another three days) was a long time to spend in a box. Gracie never complained aloud, but she eyed me pitifully, her nose stuck in my direction through the bars. When the sun beat down on her, I tried shading her with a towel, but it blocked my view of the passenger-side mirror.

Happiness is finally arriving at our favorite camping place on Cedar Key. I hope we stay here a while.

So now, when we drive to Florida, we leave the crate in the garage. Gracie sits wherever she is comfortable—in front in the sun if it's cold, or in the cool back if she's hot. Yes, she could be thrown through the windshield in an accident, but, much like my refusal of certain breast cancer treatments, it becomes an issue of quantity versus quality of life. So far, so good.

See also **Barking, Commands** and **Winter**.

Affection

Gracie wasn't especially affectionate—she rarely even looked at me. I know a dog who will, if permitted, lick my face cleaner than a plate after dinner. Not Gracie. I assumed that Gracie would eventually go bananas over me, but she never has, except after she's spent a few hours alone. She tolerates hugs and pats, but mostly she just wants her ears scratched.

If my head is covered, you can't see me, can you?

Even after two years, Gracie's not very demonstrative. She likes to burrow, often disappearing completely beneath a fleece blanket or sleeping *under* her dog bed, but should I be so rude as to reach out my arms to hug her, Gracie will beat a retreat. She may jump onto my lap when visiting friends, or curl into my body on a cold night on the road, but she will wriggle free from even affectionate constraints. I find this disconcerting.

Now well into our third year, I am sometimes treated to a little lick, especially when I'm stretched out in the RV working on this book, or first thing in the morning. At first I took this cat-like independence personally, but after I read up on Miniature Pinschers, I realized, with some relief, that it's not me. Gracie's just staying true to her breed.

I've often wondered if we've bonded, especially after that first trip in the van, when we were together 24/7. Now, I don't think about it. Gracie is still not very affectionate, but each of us likes to know where the other is. I can't imagine Gracie not lying along my leg on the futon. She rarely strays far, even when free to run on the Florida farm. Caring for Gracie's needs has become part of caring for my own.

Alpha

I have never been offered more unasked-for advice than during Gracie's and my first month together. Most of it, though helpful, was felt like criticism. I don't usually project the kind of insecurity that attracts a flood of fix-its, but people who would never think to question my parent-

Who says I can't sleep under my bed?

23

ing skills felt perfectly free to fault the way I spoke to my dog, did or didn't discipline her, what or how much I fed her, where I should or shouldn't let her sleep, how I let her ride in the van. While I recognized the good intentions, I began to resent this need so many felt to improve me.

The advice I received the day after we arrived in Florida, however, made it all worthwhile: Marie, our first host, dear friend, artist and long-time dog owner, suggested that I never let Gracie go through a door before me. This sounded so ridiculous that I ignored her counsel. A few days later, however, after we'd moved on to the Ocala horse farm, I was assured that all animals have a pecking order. "There is always an alpha," explained Pam, my critter-savvy, horse-trainer host. "Here the alpha horse is always first through the gate."

If I wanted my new little alpha to obey me, I had to teach her to let me go first. She caught on quickly. Today Gracie waits for me to go through any door, or up or down stairs. If she forgets, I just snap, BACK UP! and she scoots her little butt back like a shot. Suddenly, Gracie seemed to regard me with new respect. The advisors backed off, too, so perhaps busting first through doors helped me reclaim my own alpha persona.

Dogs, like humans, often tend toward either an alpha (leader) or a beta (follower) personality, an alpha offering a bit more of a challenge. Gracie is clearly an alpha. One web site suggested that newbies like me should avoid taking on a Min Pin, but by the time I read that, I was in for a penny, in for a pound. Perhaps our similar personalities help us understand one another. BACK UP! spoken at the front door, reminds Gracie who's boss when the exciting prospect of a walk or a visitor makes her forget her manners. And although she's often aggressive toward other alpha dogs, she gets on with most betas.

You want me to WHAT?

There's an expert online who suggests that we should not kiss our dogs, claiming that face-licking is dog language for submission: apparently, if I kiss my dog, I give up my alpha status. Instead, to signify affection, I should rub the back of her neck the wrong way. Oh hell. I like to kiss the silky head of my dog, although I rarely get doggie kisses back. Alpha used to be called master, a word now out of use, perhaps due to the unseemly implications of the feminine version. I resist some of the labels recently in vogue—as much as I love Gracie, I am not her parent. I already have a child, now six-foot-three and over forty. Gracie is my dog, and I am her owner, alpha and person.

See also **Commands** and **Socialization**.

Barking

When I moved into my house three years ago in January, I may have been the only dogless person in the neighborhood. Small dogs yapped. Big dogs woofed. As I was painting the woodwork around an upstairs window one evening, I counted nine dogs—six over the legal in-town limit—in a nearby back yard. Barking on all sides was amplified by snow. Several years later, when I got my own dog, I feared that I'd brought all that obnoxious noise into my own yard.

At first, I did. Gracie is fifteen pounds of dedicated guard dog, alert to the smallest sound and capable of barking full-grown men into a corner. She does not tolerate strangers approaching my house, RV, Subaru, or me. Sometimes I find this behavior annoying, but it's comforting, too: Gracie may not be big enough to protect me, but I will not be unpleasantly surprised. During the three years that mine was the only dogless home on the block, my car and garage were robbed twice. Since Gracie moved in, I have not been troubled.

Gracie was proving an excellent watch dog: she barked at any person or dog within smell or sight. She barked at our neighbor, a mild-mannered librarian, when he left for work on his bicycle, and, again, when he returned. But Gracie got used to the dogs around us and soon gave them no more than a fixed, silent stare.

A year of NO! cured her of barking (well, mostly) inside the house, except when someone was at the door. However, in the yard, Gracie never fails to bark at passing dogs and at our bicycling neighbor. At least she barks AT something; she doesn't just bark to bark. If she barks for more than a few minutes, I call her inside—sometimes I just need to knock on my office window. Perhaps time has simply established house rules for

Gracie. If she barked inside inappropriately, I put her out, and if she barked outside too much I put her in. After two years and about five hundred repetitions, she gets it.

I began to notice that when people walk their dogs past my house, Gracie barks her head off, but their dogs do not make a peep. I worried that my dog was badly behaved until I realized that the reverse happened when I walked Gracie: when we'd pass other dog-owners' houses, their dogs would go nuts and Gracie would strut smugly by, peeing on their lawn to let them know who's boss. Apparently Gracie will protect our home, car, or RV, but she couldn't care less about anyone else's.

Our first Florida camping trip was a test: if Gracie couldn't travel, I wouldn't keep her. Amazing Grace Animal Rescue agreed to take Gracie back if she failed.

Well, she failed. Gracie was a patient traveler, but a camping calamity. Swept from an abusive home to a shelter and then to me in the space of a week, Gracie was audibly insecure. At our RV park, she barked at everything, and I thought I'd go crazy. She barked at every person, bike, car and dog that passed the van. I couldn't shower or visit the restroom in peace because

If you come any closer, I'll BARK!

she'd bark until I returned. This racket was hard for me to bear, having been brought up on good manners. Gracie's barking bit into my freedom.

I despaired. I planned to take her back when we returned to Michigan, but by the time we got home, I couldn't. Whenever I'd think about it, I'd choke up. At one point, sobbing—I couldn't remember the last time I cried like that—I gave in. "Okay," I said to my irritating, irresistible, incorrigible dog. "Nobody's perfect."

The second winter we went to the same RV park, and Gracie was a little better. She still barked at anyone passing, or, god forbid, approaching the van, but she was quiet when I left if I covered all the windows. Although Gracie's territorial behavior had improved, I couldn't count on it. Raised to be mindful of my neighbors, I began sounding like Ms. NO! Her territorial barking was not endearing us to the some of our RV park's population. Some passersby seemed amused, calling her Tiger, Jaws, or Killer; others gave me a look similar to one I direct at a parent who is yelling at a screaming child in the supermarket. Sometimes I just wanted to cry.

The third winter, Gracie tolerated most passing bicycles and persons. Dogs were still fair game, but she'd wait quietly alone in the van until I'd return from the rest room or shower. I could even spend an evening in town, dining with friends. I noticed, with satisfied relief, that Gracie was no longer the worst-behaved dog in the park. Camping was mostly fun again.

When we returned from our first Florida trip, I purchased a

battery-powered remote control shock collar. I might have gotten a bark collar—a bark collar shocks automatically each time the dog barks—but I preferred to decide when to administer Gracie's pain doses by using the shock collar's remote control. I soon forgot about the shock collar when Gracie's yard barking was sufficiently reduced with NO! or a quick trip into the house. Dogs do bark—my neighbors' dogs bark some, too, and we accepted reasonable levels.

Back in Florida, however, I was tempted to break out the shock collar to deal with Gracie's I-see-a-dog frenzy, but, when it came right down to it, I couldn't bring myself to use it. Two years later, the shock collar remains in its box.

An early reviewer suggested a citronella spray collar, which emits a harmless blast of a scent that dogs are reputed to hate. Available online, as bark or remote-control models, the citronella collar appears to offer a gentler, though not inexpensive, option. I have not tested it, having discovered it too late for this book. Citronella refills are available—perhaps mixing the citronella liquid with water in a squirt bottle might prove an easier option.

Bathing and Grooming

When I first took Gracie to Kaybees K-9 Training & Spa, the place where I board her when I have to leave town, I took note of a dog-bath room that supplied tubs, hoses, shampoo and possibly towels for only ten dollars. Gracie, however, didn't seem to need bathing more often than a cat—catlike, she often grooms herself, along with her favorite toy, sparing me trips to the doggie salon. I'd never bathed Gracie at all until one day she rolled in some truly disgusting muck. It happened, of course, on a holiday, so when I called Kaybees in a panic, the dog-bath room was closed.

Into the basement laundry tub went the dirty dog, where, despite her aversion to water, she stoically endured a thorough sudsing with a homemade doggie shampoo I'd whipped up from a quickly Googled recipe: a few drops of blue Dawn in a small bottle of water, a mixture reportedly used to clean the victims of oil spills. It worked so well and so quickly on Gracie that, in two years, I've never used anything else, and Gracie's shiny coat has drawn more than one compliment.

Bed

One of the first things I bought for Gracie was a cushy dog bed. Gracie claimed it immediately. During the day, I put it on my living room futon which, always open, serves as my office, dinner table and TV-watching station. But what should I do about nights?

Online advisers differed on whether a dog should sleep on or next to an owner's bed. The dog trainer I consulted worried that if Gracie slept in my bed, she would have trouble with overnight boarding. So, on our first night, I placed Gracie's dog bed on an ottoman at the foot of my bed and told her to HOP IN! She did, staying there all night, but not before a long period of plaintive gazing.

We followed this routine for the two weeks before we left for Florida. In my RV, for reasons of warmth and necessity, Gracie slept under the covers near my feet. I grew fond of her

For two whole weeks, Mary made me sleep alone in my dog bed.

gentle snores and welcome body heat. She never did have a boarding problem and I was soon sleeping better than ever. Now the dog bed sits under my desk, occasionally accompanying Gracie to overnights elsewhere.

Bicycle

A year before Gracie arrived, I received a folding bicycle for my seventieth birthday. I was looking forward to teaching Gracie to ride with me, so, during her first summer, I bought her a metal basket that fit on the handlebars, but it was uncom-

It's not as easy to jump out as it looks!

fortable for both of us. A rear-seat model, purchased at another store, kept falling off. This also had to be returned. Finally, I found a variety of bicycle dog-carriers on *Amazon.com*. The padded box, which I ordered after reading extensive reviews, cost $75. It has been worth every cent. With a little difficulty, I attached the seat to the back of the bike, and, with a bit more difficulty, figured out how to secure my fifteen-pound dog with the straps.

What fun! The folding bicycle let me ride slowly and close to the ground, so I had often used it to hunt mushrooms. As the season was upon us, we took to the woods for a test run. Twice Gracie tried to leap out, sending us both to the ground, but, as we were on a sandy path, our falls were soft and short.

Gracie soon was as calm a passenger as she had been in the van. We rode around town to visit friends. We rode around the Tobico, a local nature reserve. Recently, when I suffered a bout of plantar fasciitis (a painful foot-sole condition), Gracie ran alongside the bike, getting the exercise she craved. Soon she'd learned not to veer in front of the bike, staying on one side or the other, as close to a circus trick as we have—so far, anyway—accomplished.

Boarding/Bordetella

I hated to leave Gracie overnight, but I couldn't give up out-of-town book signings, garden shows and other events if I was to afford a dog. I was lucky to have found Kaybees K-9 Training and Spa, which I called a week before my first show. To my dismay, before she could be boarded, Gracie required a Bordetella vaccination.

Huh? I soon learned that dogs who are around other dogs and share a water bowl can contract a "kennel cough" caused by a highly infectious bacteria. Before she could be safely boarded, Gracie would require not one, but a series of Bordetella doses, administered up her nose. It would be a week before the vaccine would be effective.

Several days passed before Gracie reacted to the Bordetella vaccine, wheezing and sneezing for almost a week. Within the month, two more doses were administered. Now, after that first series, once a year is enough. The vaccine is dripped into her mouth, and she has shown no further side effects.

I felt guilty about boarding Gracie, knowing that she probably spent most of my absence in a crate, but it was one of the adjustments she needed to make for me, just as I had made some uncomfortable adjustments for her. Today, although she never resists entering the facility, she is over-the-moon when I pick her up.

Sometimes I leave Gracie with friends, who tell me that, when I leave, she cries. Oddly, I've never heard Gracie cry. I've listened for her when I leave her at home, or when I leave her at Kaybees, but I still don't know what her crying sounds like.

Boats

During our first summer together, Gracie and I were invited to go sailing on a gorgeous 45-foot boat. I'm not much of a sailor myself—I can't help worrying about the sudden storms that can show up on the Great Lakes. Since Gracie resists water not served in a bowl, I wasn't sure about her either, but it was a beautiful summer day, and I said yes.

I needn't have worried about Gracie. She took to the boat immediately, tugging to explore beyond the length of her leash. Nor was she intimidated by the steep ladder into the dark space below. "Never seen a dog so fearless on deck!" exclaimed our impressed captain.

As seems to be my luck with sailing, before long a storm did blow in, fast and hard. Gracie and I retreated below, curling up together on a cushioned bench, while above us the rain lashed our hosts as they frantically hauled in the sails. Eventu-

So when are WE gonna get a boat, huh? Huh?

ally the rain stopped, and we emerged, warm and dry, to thank our dripping friends for their endurance and expertise. I'm sure Gracie would hop aboard any boat again. Dogs, they say, have short memories.

Bones and Chewies

Everyone knows that dogs love bones, and even I knew not to feed Gracie chicken bones, but none of my local supermarkets sold or would cut dog bones. For a year, the only real bone I ever gave Gracie was a slightly curved spare rib the size and shape of my index finger. I'd brought it in a doggie bag to reward her for staying quietly in my mother's Vermont apartment while Mom and I went to lunch. Worried about the white carpet, I put Gracie and her bone out on the small, enclosed, third-floor balcony.

Two minutes later, I went out to check her progress: the bone was gone! What had she done with it? It was not in the potted geranium. How could she have chewed it up that fast—she must have swallowed it!

For days, weeks even, I examined her poop for a bone or bone fragments. I felt her tummy. I checked the internet for bone-swallowing incidents. However, Gracie showed no evidence of having swallowed anything firmer than a nice piece of meat. I never did find out where the bone went.

The following winter, while again enjoying our beloved Florida horse farm, I spied, in the refrigerator, a package of sliced "marrow bones" which Pam had purchased for her dogs. Gracie was stealing these bones from her new pals, so I bought a package of six from Publix, a Florida supermarket, and kept

Okay, it's pretty big, but I can handle it.

36

them in the RV. They were a bit greasy, but just one would keep Gracie gnawing intently for at least a couple of hours.

When the bones ran out, I needed something else to keep Gracie's jaws occupied—she made short work of the "rawhide" twists and "bones" that cost up to a dollar apiece. I found the widely available, inexpensive pig's ears, apparently the real thing, disturbing and disgusting. However, if I added a piece of cooked bacon to a tin of the less expensive chewies, just one would serve as a handy distraction when guests arrived, or when she had to endure a twelve-hour day in the van.

After watching Gracie make short work of almost every chewable treat I could find, I was happy to discover the hollow, hard rubber Kong, which promised to engage her longer. I stuffed its middle with peanut butter. Gracie snatched it and took it to her bed. Five minutes later, she'd chewed off the top. Disgusted—it had cost $9.00—I did not buy another until a year later, when I noticed an "Extra-strong" Kong. This time Gracie took fifteen minutes to destroy it. Kongs may work for some dogs, but, sadly, not for mine.

Pam suggested that real beef bones from the grocers turn out to be the healthiest, most cost-effective and longest-lasting treats for Gracie. When I didn't find them at my supermarket, I checked with the butcher shops in town—we have a surprising number—and I was able to obtain, for two dollars, an eight-inch-long beef bone sliced to fit Gracie's jaws and a heavy six-inch bone. No matter—Gracie managed the big bone just fine. She gnawed on it for hours, and for hours more the next day.

The best part? Gracie will gnaw on it over and over, even after she's buried it in the garden and dug it up again.

See also **Health (Hers)**.

Car

Gracie often accompanies me in the car as I go about my errands. As we leave the house, I go over the checklist in my head (I almost always have to go back for something): sunglasses, keys, money, phone, visor, leash, poopy bags, water bottle and water dish for Gracie—a plastic wine glass or ice-cream dish fits in the cup holder of both van and Subaru.

Gracie loves my Subaru so much, the passenger-side window has become translucent with nose prints. At first, Gracie would try to jump out any door I'd open, but she quickly learned how (and how not) to behave in a car. Concerned for her safety and mine, I have enforced my car-riding rules so often and so consistently that they have became second nature:

Mary's Three Simple Car Rules For Dogs:
1. Never touch the driver.
2. Use only the front passenger door to enter and exit.
3. Don't jump out until I say OKAY!

Gracie has become so car-savvy that I can leave from the driver's side and turn my back, confident that she won't leap into traffic. I can open her passenger-side front door to attach her leash or stow a package and know that she won't bolt.

Recently Gracie learned go straight out the back-yard gate to the car parked in the driveway without dashing up the street. I never say GET IN THE CAR! an offensive command a neighbor used to shout at her children and dogs. Instead I say, brightly, HOP IN! and open the passenger door. At first, Gracie did run off. I caught her, put her in the house and drove off without her. She never bolted again—sometimes she appears to think about it, but then she remembers.

Cats, Squirrels and Mice, Oh My!

I assumed Gracie would be fine with cats—when I found her, she was running loose in a roomful of them—and so she is, if a cat ignores her and holds its ground. A cat that remains in its chair will be cautiously sniffed, but not disturbed. However, Min Pins are terriers—chasing down fleeing prey appears to be in the genes. Gracie will always chase a cat that runs.

Hardly anything thrills Gracie more than chasing a cat, squirrel, or a mouse. Gracie has chased, but never caught or bitten, a cat or another dog. She will chew on a squirrel, bird, or mouse, on the rare occasions that she catches. She's not too interested in birds, apparently aware that she can't fly. However, during a recent walk in the woods, she stopped suddenly and watched a garter snake slither right under her nose into the grass. Gracie seems to know that there are rules about how far she can go, and with what.

Clichés

Many dog sayings have become newly meaningful since I got Gracie. For a while, in the middle of writing this book, I worried I was barking up the wrong tree (I always get discouraged in the middle of a big project.) Gracie really does "wolf" her food. I may "throw a dog a bone" when I give her a chewy as I go out the door, which, knowing a bribe when she sees one, she often disdains until my return. Her metabolism makes her a "hot dog," and she habitually "dogs my steps" when I'm around the house. I hope to never understand "dog eat dog," and "dog-eared" refers to those adorable ear tips. (One of my readers thinks dog-eared means "worn out," like the chewed-up, ragged ears of dogs that get into fights.) We've all been in the doghouse from time to time. Of course, Gracie reminds me what it means to "get your back up," although her hackles are becoming less exercised. Best let sleeping dogs lie.

Coats and Sweaters

A short blue leash and a thin green polyester coat were the only accessories that came with Gracie from the shelter. My

Mary sewed my first wool coat from a red ski sweater, and I still wear it. The fleece lining is the cosiest! Now I just need ear muffs.

40

very short-haired new dog needed something warmer. A life-long sewing fiend (I'm avoiding the word sewer), I immediately traced the coat onto a big sheet of paper to get the size, and before you could say Happy New Year, Gracie was tucked into a fleece-lined, boiled-wool coat cut from an

I require a sweater when Mary sets the thermostate too low. I'm partial to turtlenecks.

This turquoise coat with a pink bow gets me a lot of attention.

up-cycled L.L. Bean Norwegian ski sweater. Although that coat is on its third winter, Gracie now has more choices.

I am always surprised at Gracie's patience with her gear. She seems to enjoy modeling her newest wardrobe for my book club members, calmly allowing me to change her leopard fleece coat for a plastic Mickey Mouse raincoat, to, say, a watch-plaid coat with silver buttons.

When my friend Mary gave me a book of dog sweater instructions,

I found a new use for my yarn stash. Before long, I'd knitted an Irish fisherman sweater, perfect for our winter indoor temperatures. Then, from a man's up-cycled boiled-wool

I'm not allowed to wear my Irish Fisherman's sweater outdoors.

sweater, I cut and sewed another, using the first knitted sweater as a pattern.

I found three problems with sweaters that I didn't have with coats: Knitted or crocheted fabrics often stretch, so a sweater may soon sag. Also, if the leg holes are too big, a front foot might get caught in one. Third, sweaters can get snagged in underbrush, so they're best worn indoors.

I've made so many doggie coats, raincoats and sweaters for friends that I may start offering the sewing patterns, or even the gear itself, on my Etsy store, *GladPlaids.com*. Check it out, as well as the many other wonderful Etsy shops that offer creative canine couture.

Commands

After I learned to enforce BACK UP! I had less trouble teaching Gracie other commands. SIT! was the next one. At first I had to push her haunches down, but, by the second day, her efforts encouraged with treats and praise, at SIT! I got a smartly plopped dog.

Then Pam encouraged me to teach Gracie to COME! so Gracie could run free on the horse farm. Teaching her this command was my first experience in risk—I had to let her run if she was to learn to COME! Watching Gracie rocket across a football-sized pasture—I didn't know she could run like that!—made me almost frantically nervous. I yelled GRACIE, COME! so much that I felt (but did not see) Pam and Jim roll their eyes. Yes, I was a slow learner, but, fortunately, Gracie wasn't. She still doesn't always COME! when called, but she does, mostly. At least she knows what it means.

LIE DOWN! was another matter. Confused between sitting and lying down, a full sprawl became Gracie's full-out kitchen begging posture when sitting and staring wasn't resulting in tidbits. It gave new meaning to the word "groveling."

As for STAY! I've counted as high as twenty while I back away, as advised by a trainer, but she just doesn't get it. Now,

SIT! you say?
You've got a treat there, right?

I say WAIT! I discovered this command when, reaching a street corner on a walk, I'd stop and say WAIT! We wouldn't continue until I said OKAY! Now she'll WAIT! on the corner, in the car, or inside an open door, but she still will not stay glued to some

43

spot that makes no sense to her just because I say so. Gracie likes training and working on commands, so perhaps we'll work on STAY! again.

I tried QUIET! to control Gracie's barking, but found it hard to say it firmly enough. Now I use SETTLE! I learned this handy command after dropping Gracie off for boarding or socialization at Kaybees, where often I was amazed at the large numbers of dogs corralled in several ringed and fenced-off areas. If the dogs became excited at Gracie's entrance, barking all at once, one of the attendants would say SETTLE! and they'd all shut up. Since Gracie was already becoming familiar with this command, I thought I would try it at home. It worked best inside the house.

While many commands have taught Gracie to *do* many things, only NO!—or a sharp HEY!—work for what *not* to do. She may ignore a NO! but she knows what it means. NO! has trained Gracie to stay inside outdoor boundaries or outside an indoor room. NO! will stop her from barking in the yard or sniffing at a fascinating pile of poop. It has proved more protection for guests or furniture than GET OFF! or GET DOWN! It has not helped with leash yanking, barking at approaching strangers or dogs, or hysterical pawing at her Subaru window when I drive pass another dog.

Although Gracie seemed to have learned little more than NO! during her first four years of life, she has already caught on to, among other commands, GO OUT! GO GET YOUR TOY! COME IN! and GO TO YOUR BED! She may not instantly obey, but two years of countless repetitions and treats have made our lives happily predictable. An old(er) dog really can learn new tricks.

See also **Advice** and **Freedom (Hers)**.

Crates

I saw my first crate—a rectangular, heavily wired box for transporting or containing an animal—at Amazing Gracie Animal Rescue. I called it a "cage," which is what it looked like, but Shawna immediately corrected me. Persons who love animals resist "caging" them, which sounds cruel. Crating feels more like a safety measure. So now I say "crate."

I've got quite a crate collection now, bought inexpensively from garage sales (new crates are not cheap). I keep thinking I might need the big one if, in some emergency, I have to leave Gracie with someone who doesn't trust her in the house. So far, I haven't needed that one, but I also have a smaller crate that straps into the front seat of the van, which I used during our second Florida trip. The third crate is a soft, canvas, collapsible number that works nicely in the Subaru, providing a cushy napping place or escape from the sun on our annual trips to Vermont. It also serves as her studio dog bed.

Dog Parks

Because Gracie can run free in our yard, we frequent the dog park mostly to help socialize her. Before I adopted Gracie,

I had never visited a dog park—a large, fenced area where dogs can run off-leash. A short drive from home, our park is divided into a small dog and a big dog yard, which we like, as Gracie is intimated by a romping passel of large dogs, even when they are friendly.

When we first visited the dog park, Gracie got along with the small dogs, but she snarled and barked through the chain-link fence at the big dogs, which snarled and barked back. Since running free with all sorts of dogs on the Florida horse farm, however, Gracie now approaches most dogs with curiosity, sniffing noses and chasing up and down the fence. This is true only if she's off-leash; on a leash, Gracie is a little less hostile if she's allowed to sniff noses and butts, but this is not a sure thing. Gracie seems most compatible with the calmer golden retrievers, collies and labs. It feels counterintuitive, but Gracie might prefer a large dog as a companion—impossible, but fun to think about.

Doorbell

Gracie reacts to our doorbell as if it were implanted in her head, exploding into a barking, pawing frenzy, leaving claw marks on our vintage woodwork—her sole destructive behavior. Despite her small size, she scares people. "Wouldn't it be great," said Kristine, my optimistic trainer, "if, when the doorbell rang, Gracie jumped into her bed without barking?"

Well, yes, it would. The idea was that, like a Pavlov dog, with training and treats, Gracie would soon leap in her bed at the sound of the bell. So I bought the battery-operated door chime Kristine suggested, tackled the clam shell packaging with a can opener, loaded four AA batteries, mounted the chime section in the entryway, carried the button into the kitchen and, finally, rang the bell—a ding-dong chime like ours.

Nothing happened. Gracie did not bark. I rang it again, and, again, no reaction. Finally, I snuck out the back door, tiptoed around the house to the front door and rang the real doorbell. Silence—Gracie knew it was me. When I finally opened the door, she practically elevated, so happy to see me. The hardware store did refund my $21.50, despite the destroyed packaging.

There's a doorbell on a TV ad that sounds even more like ours than the battery-operated one. Gracie perked up at first, but soon ignored it. Now, if she knows who is at the door, she's excited, but doesn't bark. Otherwise, the doorbell continues to inspire fury. Finding her guard-dog instincts comforting, I've decided to let this one go.

Drawings

I did thirty black-and-white watercolor pencil paintings to illustrate this book, but I ended up agreeing with my editorial readers that using photos as well really added to the flavor of the stories and meant there could be more pictures in the book.

Jenny Blair drew my portrait.

Aha! What do I see here? I'd better get busy
and relieve Mary of her kitchen-floor-cleaning chore.

Drawing Gracie has become part of our story, so I've included some of my art, which I did for the book while we were in Florida. I like the drawings much better in color—see my favorite one on the cover. My friend Jenny Blair came over one day, and, holding Gracie on her lap with one hand, drew her with

What could be better than lying in my cushy bed
grooming my lambie?

the other. Gracie is nuts about Jenny, who can draw anything. Sometimes she takes Gracie for runs and feeds her when I'm out of town. So Gracie patiently sat for her portrait.

Ears

I decided to buy my house sight-unseen after I'd looked at the three-car insulated garage with four Andersen skylights and twelve fluorescent light fixtures. It was like

Sitting for Jenny to draw me,
I am clearly the ear apparent.

that with Gracie's enormous ears—I loved them! An initial attraction like that can change a person's life.

It's hardly surprising that Gracie's ears are very sensitive—like most dogs, she hates loud noises. Our trainer has even suggested that, to emphasize a NO! I might clang some pot lids or clap. Some dogs become frightened at prolonged booming, like thunder or, in our case, fireworks.

The week before and after July Fourth, window-rattling ka-booms begin at dusk on our block. Gracie doesn't whine or whimper, but she does hang closer than usual. The first year, I

49

wondered if I should leave her alone while I biked to the river to watch Bay City's famous three-night firework displays. She didn't seem upset during the first two nights, so at ten o'clock on the third (and final) night, I rode my little folding bike to my favorite viewing spot, weaving easily through the crowds. Gracie did seem glad to see me when I got back, but she always seems glad to see me. Now every year I take off for an hour to watch our July Fourth spectacular, and every year, apparently Gracie forgives me.

A friend whose dogs freak out during thunderstorms and fireworks, upon learning that I made dog coats, wondered if I made thundershirts, reputed to calm frightened dogs. I'd never heard of a thundershirt, but I found some online: they look much like the coats I make for Gracie, but with a tighter fit. They probably feel reassuring, like the compression sleeve I once wore to prevent lymphedema after breast cancer surgery. Gracie, who habitually burrows under blankets and never resists donning a coat, perhaps finds more than just warmth in her couture.

Unlike the floppy ears on a poodle I once knew, which required daily attention, Gracie's big perky ears allow constant air circulation and resist infection. I don't clean her ears unless they irritate her. Gracie prefers having her ears scratched to any other form of affection. Sometimes, to get my attention, she goes at them with a hind foot, which makes her look like a rabbit. She can even give herself a head scratch!

Recently I met a Min Pin with floppy ears. The owner informed me that the ears of some Min Pins have been cropped to make them stand up. Some Min Pins' ears are erect on their own, which I hoped was the case with Gracie, especially when I learned that the painful procedure required not only surgery, but six weeks to six months of taping. Ear-cropping is outlawed as unnecessarily painful in some countries, but not in the United States.

I've tried to interpret Gracie's ear positions, guessing that laid back ears signal resistance, discomfort, or fear. Swiveled to the side seems to show irritation or impatience, and pricked forward, full alert. A horse's ear action looks similar to me. And yes, Gracie's ears stay up when she sleeps.

Expenses

If I'd thought of it, I could have searched the internet for "dog care costs," but I'm glad that, as I looked for a dog, I was still living in the past, when shelters were so happy to release a dog that you paid a small fee and off you went. I might have been discouraged by today's pet expenses: fees at adoption agencies often range from $75.00 to $250.00 to cover the cost of neutering, vet bills, food, space maintenance, heat, personnel and other expenses.

Gracie's unusually low adoption fee of $75 was just the beginning of this frisky new budget category. On our way home, I stopped at a box store, rushing to make my purchases lest my yet-unnamed dog chew on or stink up my Subaru. I returned to an undamaged vehicle with dog food ($20), a plush dog bed

($35), a Flexie retractable leash ($15) and a dog toy ($7). Since then, I have spent more on dog treats than on dog food, boarded Gracie during longer trips and art show weekends (a minimum of $23), and, despite her excellent health, spent more on Gracie's docs and meds than I did on my own. It's not cheap to take good care of a dog. (A friend once confessed she'd spent more on her dogs than her kids.)

A dog, however, can be worth the effort and expense, a memorable addition to the life of a person, family, child, or older adult: a lesson in responsibility and source of companionship. This is now true for me: although I wince at each new bill, I just pay up. If budget adjustments must be made, I find a way. Funding my dog feels no different than maintaining my car, my house and my Synthroid prescription.

Eyes

"I can always tell by their eyes what kind of dog they are," said my psychic best friend, peering into Gracie's poppy eyes on my dog's first day with me. I worried about the verdict: Gracie's were not the trusting eyes of a golden retriever or the eager eyes of a hound. To me, her dark marble-like eyes looked scared, alert and cautious. Mary never shared what she saw in Gracie's eyes that day, but she's become Gracie's favorite fan.

For months, Gracie wouldn't look at me at all. Now she frequently fixes me with an urgent stare. But what does she want? Food? Out? Walk? Play? Sometimes I get it, sometimes not. I still can't read much from Gracie's eyes.

Min Pins may be prone to eye problems, but, so far, Gracie only experiences an occasional discharge from an inside corner, which hardens into a quarter-inch crust. She patiently tolerates the warm wet cloth I use to wipe it off.

Fleas, Ticks and Heartworm

I've only found one tick on Gracie—a tiny, grayish, eight-legged dot, which I recognized from the few ticks I have pulled off myself. My animal-savvy friend Pam happened to be handy, so I watched her pull the tick out, head and all, with her fingernails. "That's not the official way to remove a tick," Pam said, "but this way I can feel whether I've gotten the head out."

I found some alternative tick-removal methods online. Before our spring tick season arrives, I'll purchase one of the tick-removal tools available on Amazon or eBay. I already have tweezers narrow enough to grab the tick head (not the body). If I have to use my fingernails, I will, as suggested, protect myself from the bacteria with a tissue or gauze. I'll kill removed ticks in a small bottle of rubbing alcohol or in the freezer.

DO NOT, I learned, try to kill an imbedded tick with alcohol or a match, as that may induce the intruder to release its bacteria. Good to know, as that's exactly how I used to do it.

I've used Frontline Plus liquid every month on my cringing dog, scraping the plastic applicator through the fur on the back of her neck. She doesn't like it, but I have never noticed fleas on her, in the house, or in the RV. (An exception might be a recent episode on the farm, when all the dogs suddenly began scratching themselves; we treated them all with a spray recommended by Pam's veterinarian.) Gracie's reward for tolerating the flea treatment is a chewable Heartgard Plus pill. This she gobbles right down. Heartworm, for which Gracie is tested annually, is a not uncommon, life-threatening condition.

Flea and heartworm preventatives are essential but ridiculously expensive—I feel like a dupe every time I write the big check for a six-month supply. To ease the pain, in my head I break the amount into the weekly cost to keep house and occupants varmint-free, and it doesn't hurt quite so much.

Recently—too late to test for this book—I discovered a recipe for a "natural" flea powder, apparently "chemical-free." A "flea powder for dogs" internet search led to several promising do-it-yourself possibilities. A disadvantage with powders is the need to re-apply them after a treated dog gets wet. Still, avoiding the chemicals and the outrageous expense might be worth the effort.

Food

What and how much I should feed my dog is still not entirely clear to me. Our adoption agency suggested 4-Health dry dog food, which Gracie had been fed during her stay there. When I arrived at Tractor Supply—my first visit to the only chain that seems to sell the brand—I discovered six varieties, with

Is it dinnertime?
Is it dinnertime?

54

and without grain. I bought a five-pound bag of each. To avoid boring Gracie, I fed her a half-cup of, say, trout and potato for breakfast and a half-cup of chicken and rice for dinner. In between, she got one-third cup of treats, which often included bites of cheese, chicken, or whatever I was making for dinner.

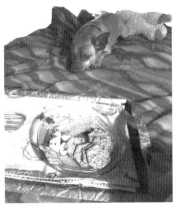

Hurry up! Eating fast is good for your health.

About a month later, a person who clearly knew more about dogs than I did expressed horror at the amount I was feeding Gracie. "That's far too much!" she exclaimed. So I reduced Gracie's food to one-third cup twice a day plus one-third cup of treats, a total of one cup. Six months later, Gracie had lost two pounds, one-seventh of her body weight—no wonder she was always hungry! I'd have to lose twenty-one pounds to equal it. So we went back to a scant half-cup twice a day with treats and tidbits in between, and that seems to keep her weight around fifteen pounds. The dog people insist I should be able to see her ribs under her coat, and I can, mostly.

"Dogs aren't like people," I was assured by an amused shelter volunteer upon hearing how I so thoughtfully varied Gracie's meals. "They don't care about variety." So now I feed her the same thing morning and night and only change up the flavor with a fresh bag. I never leave food in her bowl, as many dog owners do, as Gracie is not one to pace herself—when we visit homes where other dogs are supplied with endless chow, Gracie wolfs down everything in sight. Lengthy visits can result in serious pooping and weeks of cutbacks.

If I wanted to get seriously confused, I could start worrying about grains: anxiety over grains in dog food has fomented quite the online controversy. I relieved my mind, and saved time, by looking up Gracie's 4-Health kibble on *DogFoodAdvisor.com*, where, along with hundreds of competing brands, it was carefully reviewed and the contents meticulously analyzed.

Gracie is not a picky eater. She dances for her dry food (which came in at four stars) every morning and, again, about half an hour before her dinner time. This simple, inexpensive routine has reliably maintained her health and weight. Does Gracie ever get dog food from a can? You're kidding, right?

I never knew that even a small amount of chocolate could kill a dog until, many years ago, a friend lost her beautiful Afghan hound when it got into some chocolate. To this day I worry that I may have said something insensitive, as she has hardly spoken to me since. Gracie loved the scent of Dove foil wrappers, which seduced her into a rare episode of wastebasket diving. I take extra care to keep chocolate in a closed drawer, at least when I'm not consuming it.

Gracie loves all kinds of my own food—apples, bananas, cheese, meat—so I checked the A.S.P.C.A. web site so I would know what people foods that might be harmful. Now, in addition to obvious no-nos like chicken and other splinter-prone bones, I never offer Gracie avocados, grapes or raisins, beer (hops), bread dough, alcohol, macadamia nuts, moldy food, garlic or onions, foods with the sweetener Xylitol, or, of course, anything toxic to people.

Freedom

Gracie's first concern upon entering a new space is, as my friend Fran puts it, "securing the perimeter." This entails sniffing the baseboards in every room, or, outside, every inch of fence. If there is a way to escape, Gracie will find it.

So I always worry about leaving Gracie in a new yard, lest she find herself in strange territory. My concern was confirmed one dark, winter evening when, assured that there were no holes in our host's fence, I let Gracie out in the back yard. When I called her back in, she had disappeared into the night. Fresh snow had fallen during dinner, so I followed her little footprints across the often-busy street to a chain-link fence, through which Gracie was sniffing the nose of a beagle.

In time, Gracie has come to respect most boundaries, but only if I've taken the trouble to teach her where they are. Each time we arrive on the farm in Florida, where widely-spaced post-and-board fencing encloses the farm and corrals the horses, I walk Gracie off-leash around the property line several times, firmly saying NO! each time she tries to cross it. Then I can trust her to stay on the farm, even with the gate open.

Back home, I've begun teaching Gracie to STAY! inside the

I'm off the leash at last! Now to explore the stables.
Do I smell cats in there?

open gate while I roll the trash can down our long driveway to the curb. I've repeated this chore weekly six times so far, and already she no longer tries to follow me. In a few more weeks, I won't need to look over my shoulder.

How much freedom I can give my dog also depends on where we are. When we travel, except in friends' houses, yards, or farms, Gracie's outdoor life is spent on a leash, or attached to the RV by a line. I'd like to train her to walk with me off-leash, but we're not quite there yet.

It bears repeating: With trust comes freedom. Gracie got the run of my messy house as soon as I realized that I could trust her not to touch anything I didn't give her. After she learned to COME! she could play off-leash on the farm. It's been hard for me to resist becoming a helicopter dog owner, and I still find that early stage of some training nerve-racking. Yes, she's bolted, but every time, it's been worth it. In the end, increasing Gracie's freedom also increases mine.

See also **Commands**.

Grass

Gracie needs grass. During the rare times she has wakened me in the wee hours, she's gone out to eat grass. Grazing has been a sure sign of an upset stomach. In winter, when our lawn disappears beneath snow, Gracie suffers a constipated adjustment period. Except in extremity, Gracie will poop only on grass. When we drive south in winter, and I scan the landscape for signs of green, it's not just to raise my spirits.

Of course, there's the unpleasant pick-up preparation for mowing the lawn, a task, like vacuuming, I already hate. Each time I don the disposable gloves—I often use a poopy bag—I chide myself for not having trained Gracie to go behind the shed, the way my mother trained my brother's dog to "perform" at the far end of the property. Now, I pay for my early neglect, careful to get out there before the grass gets so high that it hides the offenders.

We really miss our fenced back yard when we're not home.

Grass!

The RV offers little room for Gracie to do more than sit or sleep; except for visits to the horse farm, she lives on leash and line. When, after several months away, I pull into our home driveway, get out and close the gate, Gracie joyfully reclaims her personal patch of grass. At last she can chase squirrels, laze in the sun and poop and pee at will. The scarcity of off-leash opportunities for Gracie is one of our obstacles to full-time RVing. Although I chose the RV over world travel so I could have a dog, the dog gives up something, too.

Guests and Friends

Gracie welcomes all but our most frequent guests with barking and jumping. The chaos used to continue through the foyer and into the house, while I apologized and told Gracie to GET DOWN! I tried leaving treats outside the front door with which our guests could befriend Gracie, an effective ploy that backfired, turning her into an obnoxious beggar.

Now, I try to be prepared when I expect guests. When they enter the house, I tell Gracie to GO TO YOUR BED! As this always involves a chewy, she can't get there fast enough. Her attention diverted, she soon calms down. In time, Gracie has become familiar with friends who make frequent appearances, and the problem has mostly solved itself. If she's not sure who it is, she still makes a ruckus, but that's her job.

At the dinner table, with or without guests, Gracie waits patiently for me to finish eating, unless conversation goes on beyond endurance, or I am slow to clean my plate. Then I might be reminded, with a crescendo of sneezes, that it's her turn. I confess (a warning to future dinner guests) that I let Gracie lick a plate on its journey to the dishwasher. Although most dog owners don't seem to mind, some friends are appalled. I enjoy rewarding Gracie's patience with this simple indulgence, from which she derives such reliable joy.

Training Gracie may have been easier for me as the sole resident of the house. Almost all of my friends support my efforts; the few that don't are not Gracie's alpha, so she mostly ignores them, or soon forgets. Even so, it takes an effort to be consistent, which, with repetition and, of course, treats, results in at least some measure of success. Getting an entire family to train a dog consistently must be a challenge. If I should ever share my space with another person, we will have to agree on how to deal with the most common doggie situations.

Health (hers)

Small dogs often enjoy longer lives with fewer serious health problems than many of the larger breeds. Min Pins are a healthy breed and can live to fifteen years. That gives us at least ten years if all goes well: I have a good chance of living long enough to take care of her, and she'll probably live long enough to keep me company. Still, health can be an issue with a dog, especially a new one.

Soon after I brought Gracie home she began to noisily lick her butt and slide it across the orange and yellow striped rug my father brought me from Haiti thirty years ago. I found the sound annoying, especially at night. Also, I was worried: did she have worms? The vet informed me that, especially in small dogs, sometimes fluid, which is normally expelled by defecating, collects in sacs on either side of the anus. Two minutes (and $20) later, he had cleared it out with a lubricated finger and some gauze.

Yike. Would I have to do this procedure myself? I didn't relish choosing between the off-putting task or frequent twenty-dollar vet visits. Fortunately, when Gracie began eating and exercising normally, producing bigger and firmer poops—I now notice these things—extended butt-lapping has become rare.

I also worry that Gracie will break a bone doing circus jumps in and out of the van, traversing furniture by air, or crashing through brush after a squirrel. Although Gracie's built like a sack of sugar, she has oddly delicate legs. She's not cautious about her legs, but she's fussy about her little feet, limping piteously after stepping on a burr or a bead of snow. When I see her hopping on one or two legs, the rest disabled, I am quick to the rescue. Fortunately, she's tougher than she looks and has never fractured a bone.

I've been lucky in the two years I've had Gracie, aged four when I got her, now six. Small emergencies, like shortness of breath after too much excitement, have worked themselves out at home. A Min Pin's normal well-being may encourage this happy state, as well as our regular health maintenance.

See also **Thief!**

Health (Mine)

I've experienced both sides of the dog-owner's health debate. The arguments against owning a dog warn of accidents and falls, a special concern for older adults like me. My first health event occurred five minutes after leaving Amazing Grace Animal Rescue: I put my new dog in the back seat of my Subaru and prayed that she would neither have nor cause an accident. A few minutes down the road, she began struggling toward the front. When I reached back to push her into the passenger seat, I instantly sustained a rotator cuff injury.

What was I thinking? I should have brought a crate or at least a friend to hold a dog, should I find one. Putting a strange dog into my car with no restraints was nuts. Two visits to my rheumatologist, a shot of cortisone, three hours of ice packs and a Medicare bill later, I survived my first accident.

A week later, I put Gracie in the van, and, on my way to the driver's side, I slipped on a patch of ice and slammed, face first, into the concrete. Stunned, my mouth full of grit, I lay there for a long time, terrified that I'd broken my jaw and crushed all my front teeth. When I managed to stagger into the house, the face in the bathroom mirror horrified me: with even just a front tooth broken in half, I looked, and felt, like a car-crash survivor. (I have been a car-crash survivor, and I know.) Completing the effect were a bruised jaw and two black eyes.

Eighteen months later, walking Gracie home from a dinner party and distracted by an approaching dog, I fell, sideways, off a curb onto the street. Two women, who'd been watching from a nearby porch, came running, helped me up after I caught my breath and offered to take me home. Relieved that all my limbs were working, I thanked them and continued on alone. A week and two X-rays later, I discovered I'd fractured three ribs.

I have fully recovered from all three accidents, the only reminder a faint line across my left front tooth and an occasional twinge on my right side. I have become more careful.

One of my favorite authors, nutritionist Jane Brody, described her own experience adopting a dog in her lengthy April 8, 2014, *New York Times* Wellness Blog: "Life With a Dog." Her circumstances—a writer, my age, living alone—sounded similar to mine. Like other pro-dog people, she cites the many studies reporting increased dog-owner longevity, health and happiness, as well as the social advantages to older adults.

In my case, just consider the exercise: Although I've hunted mushrooms for twenty years, I have added to those mostly-fall hikes the "moderate exercise" touted in medical journals. Gracie makes me laugh at least five times a day, laughter adding another scientifically proven health benefit. I'd never expected to be so happy, healthy and contented in my eighth decade.

I have even lost weight. I'd been trying, unsuccessfully for years, but in six months of walking Gracie, I lost five pounds. I was on a roll, so I asked a visiting friend, who was looking unusually trim, about her 5:2 diet: She limited calories to 500 two days a week, she said, but ate whatever she wanted the other five. You had to love a diet that could be summarized in a sentence! Online instructions were easily obtained and free. After I saw a PBS program about the 5:2 diet, I was a convert. In six months I lost twenty-five pounds, shrank two jeans sizes, and I looked ten years younger (or so I was told, more than once). I certainly felt it: Gone was the acid reflux that had kept me awake at night for years. Gone was the pain in my knees. Now, when we walk, I can almost keep up with Gracie.

Pet adoption can be a risk, but long ago, in my mid-thirties, I made a conscious decision to stop letting what-ifs stop me from pursuing my heart's desires. I've trusted my instincts—what I regard as my feminine side—counting on my rational side to make my choices work. My child, friends, lovers, travel, adventures, writing, art—and adopted dog—have not come free, but the rewards have made price irrelevant.

Hotels/Motels

The few times we've stayed in a hotel or motel, Gracie has not barked or marked, but I've never dared leave her alone there. Friends who frequently travel with their dogs told me how they trained them to stay quiet. "The first time, we closed the door and waited right outside," they said. "When the dogs barked, we said NO! and waited again, each time moving farther away."

I don't know how long it took, but if I had to travel this way, I'd take whatever time we needed to teach Gracie hotel etiquette. For Gracie, however, learning to feel secure in strange environments seems mostly a matter of feeling secure with me.

The longer we're together, the more quickly she seems to adapt to my temporary absences.

My traveling friends use *bringfido.com* and *Officialpethotels. com* to find pet-friendly accommodations.

House Manners

I was nervous the first time I left Gracie home alone. When I returned, she greeted me as if I were returning from a long tour of duty. A brief house inspection found nothing disturbed. The next time I left for an evening. Again, I was welcomed with joy. One day I had to do a show in a nearby town and arranged for a friend to stop by to feed and walk her. The friend forgot and Gracie went ten hours without a break. Still, I could find no telltale spots or stains.

I may be unusually fortunate—Gracie even stays out of the kitchen trash. Despite showing little evidence of formal training, Gracie could not have been better mannered if she'd been trained by Queen Victoria or my mother. There are exceptions: She of-

There's a dog out there! There's a dog out there!

66

ten perches on the dining room chair or even on the table to see out the window, although never when I'm home. Just today, returning from a solo errand, I found a water glass on its side, the tablecloth soaked! Gracie!

Immunizations and Preventatives

Gracie was up to date on her required immunizations when I adopted her, but after a year, she needed her annual DHLP-PV-CV shot, which protects against distemper, hepatitis, leptospirosis, parainfluenza and parvovirus. Each of these diseases can cause illness, possibly death, and are highly contagious. I have to update her canine rabies shot every three years. I could never keep track of these if my veterinarian didn't remind me by e-mail and print the dates of her last immunization updates at the bottom of each receipt.

See also **Boarding/Bordetella**.

Insecurity/Security

At first, Gracie was a very insecure dog—almost anything could set her off barking and jumping. Mine has been at least her third home, possibly her fourth or fifth. I'll never know what made her cringe from my hand or snarl at approaching male friends, but I can try to make her present life fairly predictable, even as we adventure into new environments.

With this in mind, I have tried to develop routines: one for home in summer, another for winter, and a third for the RV.

Each time we switch, we endure an awkward transition period, but soon life becomes once again, comfortably predictable.

I think these routines have helped Gracie feel secure. Wherever we are, breakfast is always upon rising, dinner will appear at four and we'll walk every day unless prevented by the weather, illness, or my sore feet. Visitors will reliably treat her kindly. Now, although she still welcomes me from a few hours' foray without her as if I'd been abroad, she seems to know that I always come back.

Structure has been a good thing, like the outline I made for this book—an intrinsic order that inspires creativity. Gracie routinely sits for treats, plops herself anywhere I pat my hand, and extends her nose to receive a doggie coat when she sees me pick one up. Routines give us time to regroup and prepare for our next challenge, which is, no doubt, at this moment approaching at warp speed, just out of sight.

After two years, Gracie seems less wary. Time, repetition, routine, reliable kindness and the hundreds of times I have returned seem to have settled her. "Gracie seems more mature," comment my friends, who dote on her. At six years old, she has found a safe place in the scary scheme of things.

Joy

Charles Schulz must have owned a dog—how else could he have perfectly captured Snoopy's happy dance? Gracie replicates it each time I reach for the dog food, arrive home, or put on my walking shoes. Her exuberance teaches me to appreciate the gift of the ordinary. Five minutes of fetch, a bit of ham, a half-hour walk, a ride in the car, or a fleece to burrow in will inspire joy. Gracie knows what's important.

Kitchen

Gracie has practically worn a spot on the hooked rug I brought home from Hawaii one year, upon which she plants her butt and waits for tidbits, nose raised like a baby bird's. Gracie can hear from upstairs the sound of the refrigerator door opening, the crackle of a plastic bag, or the *foop* of a lid lifting off a canister. The sound of a chef's knife doing it's job or a frying pan hitting the burner will bring her out of a deep snooze. A rotisserie chicken emerging from its plastic egg is enough to lure her in from behind the garage.

I am indulgent with my dog. Although I only feed her dry dog food, I am liberal with bits from the cutting board. If it's

I know this isn't my kitchen, John,
but can I please please have a piece of that cheese?

cheese or chicken or fish or meat, Gracie will prostrate herself, her raised eyes filled with hope and pleading for more, but she will accept bits of apple or pear.

It's not just in my kitchen. When we visit friends, should

someone be making dinner, Gracie will instantly abandon me to hang out with the cook. She may even get underfoot in her friendly eagerness. Dogless owners don't always know what to make of Gracie's urgent begging by the stove, but the dog people do. Whether she is rewarded or ignored depends on the

Share time!

local house rules.

Leashes

The first leash I bought for Gracie was a Flexie, a hard plastic handle enclosing a retractable line that could be released to any length up to fifteen feet. When I walked Gracie on the Flexie, she would dash to the end of

That Flexie line frayed and broke!

the line and yank, misjudging its length. Our trainer did not approve of Flexies, but I was convinced that it allowed Gracie a lot of freedom and fun, so I continue to use it.

One day, as we walked in a park, Gracie lunged so hard at a German shepherd that the Flexie line, which had badly frayed, broke. Fortunately, the big dog remained calm, and I was able to pick up Gracie before harm could be done. When I apologized and expressed amazement at the German shepherd's composure, the owner told me his dog was wearing a shock collar and showed me the remote. "It worked quickly," he said. "You should try it."

When we got home, I e-mailed the Flexie company, which agreed to replace the broken leash. Meanwhile, I didn't buy a shock collar (yet), but I did order a bright-yellow, six-dollar leather leash on eBay. From the time it arrived two days later, that leash has been a daily part of our lives. At last, I understood why a six-foot leather leash was preferred by my trainer: I finally had

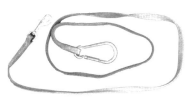

What could be better than seeing Mary pick up my leather leash?

control of my dog! Holding the leash in my right hand, I could use my left to shorten or lengthen it, impossible with the thin Flexie line. Its shorter length kept Gracie manageably close and there were no more mad dashes to the end.

Two years later we are using the same leather leash, with the addition of a heavy carabiner on the looped end. The new Flexie, which arrived weeks later, still lies, unused, in its box.

I first noticed a carabiner at the veterinarian's office, where it was installed beneath the counter so pet owners could hook on a leash and use both hands to write the check. An entire year went by before I realized how useful it was and

Mary slipped a big carabiner to her end of my leash!

bought some for myself. Now carabiners have become indispensable, transforming a length of rope into a leash that I can quickly clip around a fence rail, telephone pole, or post. Although I have several sizes of carabiners, I keep an extra-large one attached to my end of Gracie's leather leash, making it easier to hold and turning it into a potential weapon should I ever need one.

Like sailors, dog owners call ropes "lines." Gracie could not tolerate RVing without her line, attached to a door hinge, length varying by available space. When I have to restrain Gracie on a line, I check her often—a space without obstacles is hard to find—she may have wound herself around a tree or a picnic table. This year I bought a bright orange water-resistant rope, which weathered better than had our white cotton clothesline. Imbedded with tiny reflectors, it also helped prevent stumbles in the dark.

We once visited a friend who lacked an escape-proof yard. To allow Gracie more running room, he hooked a short line to Gracie's collar and the other end to a high wire stretched between clothesline posts. The carabiner with which he attached Gracie's line slid smoothly along the length of the wire, making an instant dog run.

See also **Walking**.

Love

One day I was sitting at Jakes, a friendly neighborhood establishment where Gracie is often welcomed, when a man I didn't know announced that he'd just come from giving his golden retriever a bath. "That dog hates baths," he told us, "but, on command, he'll still jump right in the tub." To me he said, "I can tell you love your dog."

I told him how I was supposed to be an alpha to my dog. "Make her let me go through doors first and such."

"Bull," said the guy. "All that matters is love."

I wasn't sure I agreed with that, but it was refreshing to receive such unqualified approval.

I've often wondered, however, when I observe a well-loved dog, whether all that care would not have been better spent on a child. It's bothered me for years that animals are often treated better than many kids. Dealing with that concern, I've decided that I do not diminish the love in the world by what or whom I care for. There have been, and still are, many loves in my life. Gracie is now one of them.

Even when it comes to animals, we don't love them all equally, points out Hal Herzog, a psychology professor at Western Carolina University. He explores our inconsistent, complicated attitudes in his book with the provocative title, *Some We Love, Some We Hate, Some We Eat: Why It's So Hard to Think Straight About Animals* (Harper, 2010).

I've always preferred big dogs. Forty-some years ago, my husband and I took on two collies, and I confess to have fantasized about purchasing a well-trained German shepherd. But did I want a big dog now? Fortunately, despite being small, Gracie turns out to be a good pick for me. Even her size works—solid enough to feel like a real dog, but small enough to pick up if I have to. As an older owner, I might trip over her, but she's not going to knock me down.

Frustrated by Gracie's aggression to other dogs and her emotional reticence, I researched the breed to learn whether the problem lay with me or the dog. The answer was probably both: Min Pins are often too stubborn and aggressive for new dog owners, suggests one web site. They commonly pull at the leash and "are not overly demonstrative."

Nevertheless, we Min Pin people often develop brand loyalty. Min Pins can be adventurous, alert, curious, playful and smart. I have discovered other attractive Min Pin traits: happy but not hysterical energy, friendliness toward people and patience with confinement in a van, car, or crate. I've met several owners who, after losing a Min Pin, sought out another.

When I first got Gracie, she never wagged her stubby two-inch tail. I assumed this was a size problem, but after a few months, I noticed a little wag anticipating breakfast, a treat, or a walk. Even so, unlike dogs with energetic frond- or whip-like tails, Gracie's remains modestly expressive.

A Min Pin's tail is traditionally docked early in life, a procedure thought by the authorities to improve the breed's lines. Like ear-cropping, tail-docking requires surgery under anesthesia and is usually performed during the first nine weeks. I like the results, but I'm glad I didn't have to make the decision. Tail-docking has been banned in some countries, but not in the United States.

Look at me on the dock there. THAT is a Min Pin stance.

I have no papers identifying Gracie as purebred, but several people claiming to be experts have pronounced her a credit to her kind. She really has a classic Min Pin stance: If Gracie senses something unusual ahead, she may strike a pose worthy of the Westminster Kennel Club Dog Show—ears alert, nostrils flared, front legs planted, back legs stretched behind. She may even lift a front paw, stretch her nose forward and point. The stance shows off her muscular build and has impressed more than one observer. She also has a Min Pin's cropped ears and tail. Gracie, however, is not headed for stardom—except, of course, as the star of this book. Anyway, she shows little interest in dogs that appear on my TV.

Despite my ignorance of breeds, my Min Pin and I seem to

be enviably compatible. If I were to adopt another dog, however, this time I would do some research. With so many rescue and adoption agencies online today, offering excellent search tools, I could find almost any breed, size and age combination. If I were acquiring a dog for a child, I would check its breed tendencies—some breeds (not Min Pins) tend to be more tolerant of children than others.

See also **Alpha** and **Ears**.

Nipping

I'm at wit's end to cure Gracie of nipping—an infrequent but disquieting behavior. If someone approaches us on the sidewalk, walking fast or running, rarely, but without warning, Gracie will whip her head around and nip a passing leg on the calf. A horse farm worker, striding past our van, complained that Gracie had nipped at her heels. Fortunately, Gracie's never bitten anyone or even perforated their clothing—she seems to know to the millimeter how far she can close her jaws. When she leaps for a piece of meat, I sometimes feel her teeth graze my fingers, but she always stops in time.

Perhaps she is herding, or, like the terrier she is, hot in pursuit. Perhaps she is protecting me from strangers whose rapid appearance appears to be an attack. Whatever—it can't be allowed. These are the only times I've been tempted to strike her. I would try a shock collar, but the occasions are rare and happen too quickly to prevent.

Nose

While I've long been aware that bloodhounds have sensitive noses, I never realized how much any dog's sense of smell wildly bests mine. I pride myself on my discriminating schnoz, as my plastic surgeon father used to call it. Dad loved noses, having reconstructed hundreds of them during his long career. Did he know that the typical human nose's five million scent receptors adds up to only a fraction of a dog's 125 million to 300 million?

No wonder Gracie takes in the world through her nose. It's scentsational! Out walking, she sniffs the ground. In the car she sticks her nose out the window, not, I've learned, to feel the wind, but to "watch" the scent-ery. Gracie probably even detects my adrenaline—how else could she know, well beforehand, that I am going out, whether or not she can come along, or when someone is coming for dinner?

My friend Pam tells me that her dog Biskit can tell not only that she's going out, but whether she's likely to take him, by which shoes she puts on. Barn shoes—he beats a path to the door. Casual shoes—he may get to go in the car, so he sticks close. Dress shoes? He doesn't get up from his bed.

Odors

I don't find Gracie smelly at all, even with her infrequent bathing. After a night under warm blankets, she smells like pancakes or French toast. My nose does wrinkle at Gracie's occasional farts, but the worst odors emanate from Gracie and her cushy dog bed when they return from a night or two at a boarding facility. A few hours outdoors gets Gracie back to her sweet self, but before the reeking dog bed can retake its place under my computer desk, it must spend a night outdoors or go for a whirl in the basement laundry.

We may just be lucky—Gracie's cast iron plumbing is not necessarily typical of her breed—a Min Pin owner I met last year complained that her Min Pin emitted unbearable gas after eating almost anything.

Patience (Hers)

I am amazed at Gracie's patience with me. She's at my heels when I come and go to my back yard studio, or when I traverse the stairs. She lies under my desk when I'm at the computer, at my feet, or leans against my leg when I'm reading, watching TV, or napping. Unless she feels sick, she does not wake me at night. The only attention Gracie daily demands—dancing, scratching, shaking, or jumping on top of me—is that I walk her every day, play fetch with her toys and dish out her scant half-cup of chow on time. I marvel at the many ways Gracie has

I need to save Mary from her computer

78

managed to shape her day to mine. It's hard to remember that she spent twice as much time with someone else as she has with me.

Gracie has her limits. If she could get rid of anything in my life, it would

Enough TV already!

be my computer and television screens. I lavish most of my time and focus on these backlit rectangles. Gracie, at this moment, is positioned behind my desk chair vigorously scratching herself. She's impatient at last: it's eighty degrees in May! Why am I not outdoors, mushroom hunting in the woods, or exploring new sidewalks? Fed up with hours of waiting, she will install herself between me and the object of my attention. At last, I sigh and rise from my labors. The real world awaits us.

Patience (Mine)

I don't easily let a dependent into my life. Twice married and once a mom, I spent my early adult life responsible for others. It was said I could do the work of six people, and, often, I probably did. By my early thirties, I was a public library director with a staff of twenty, going home to a husband, six boarders (it was the commune era), two dogs, four cats, a Boston fern, ten potted geraniums and a baby. Everyone, including myself, assumed I could manage all that sweet as pie, but we were wrong. I became crabby enough for comment. In the end, I threw out the bath water, but not the baby.

After a bout of clinical depression and one more try at marriage, I resisted all potential dependents except my son. After he left home, not even a house plant would constrain my freedom. That explains why my friends and family were so dubious when I adopted a time-consuming, walk-insisting, always-with-me dog. If I wanted a pet, wouldn't a cat have been better? Where would I find the patience for such an intrusion?

I almost didn't. Thank goodness I changed my mind. I did need patience to deal with Gracie's more intractable behaviors, but I found that, like love, the more of it I used, the more I seemed to have.

Pee

From day one, Gracie didn't poop, pee, or chew in the house proper, but, the first time she had to transit the back porch to go out, she installed a big pee stain on the oriental rug next to the single bed I keep there for my son. That evening, she peed on another oriental rug in my garage-turned-studio.

I remembered the animal repellent I bought the year before to stop a neighbor's pug, allowed to run free, from killing my front yard shrubs. "Use sparingly," the hardware salesman had warned. Whew! Just a tiny dribble of the stuff nearly blew me out the back porch! I cautiously sprayed the spots in the studio as well, hoping the powerful odor would air out before spring. It did, as did the porch, and Gracie never re-peed either place, but I'll never use that stuff inside again.

Did little dogs pee more often than big dogs? At first I wondered how often to let her out. It was January, so I couldn't just leave her in the yard, and Gracie offered few indications that she had to "go." I hung a bell on the kitchen door, but she never touched it. She rarely looked uncomfortable, nor did she race to the door after an eight-hour night. So I let her out every few hours, or when I thought of it.

For almost two years, Gracie made do with my guesswork. Now, finally, she stands purposefully at the kitchen door. If I'm in another room, she stands politely where I can see her and fixes me with an urgent stare. If I still don't get it, she vigorously scratches herself, jingles her tags, or, if I'm napping, jumps on my chest. This means NOW!

At my house, six doors must be opened and closed for every Gracie round trip to the yard. So, as soon as the weather warmed, I purchased a dog door. On the off chance that I should someday get a bigger dog, I chose the medium-sized option. I don't think I could have installed it myself, but my handyman got the job done without difficulty.

Gracie took to her door immediately, first nosing through with caution, soon rocketing in and out. All summer long Gracie comes and goes as she pleases. Although I worry about an intruding skunk, to my knowledge, no critter larger than a mouse has taken advantage of Gracie's private entrance.

Playing

Gracie does not play with other dogs, but there have been two notable exceptions. The first was thanks to my friends Brenda and Allan Brouillet, who have owned dogs for their entire 30-or-more-year marriage and from whom I have received much good advice. Because of Gra-

Harkin is my "Buddha dog."

cie's hostility to other dogs, however, I was worried when, halfway into our first year, they decided to visit us, along with their beagle, Harkin. It probably helped that they brought Gracie a tooting dog toy, but we were still amazed when Gracie, without even a WOOF! welcomed Harkin into her yard, house and dog bed. She let Harkin play with her toys and drink from her water bowl. Harkin gave me hope that Gracie might someday make friends with other dogs.

During our second year, after a short period of hackles, growling and marking, Gracie learned to get along with Biskit, a terrier smaller than herself that Pam had adopted shortly after our first visit to the farm. By our third year, Gracie shared the house with Biskit, as well as another rescue, Gypsy. Gracie ran free with dogs of all sizes without fear of harm to them or to herself, although too much friskiness could still upset her.

There has been another endearing exception: Just into our second year at our Florida RV park, Gracie fell in love with a look-alike dog about twice her size named Beck. Every morning, upon seeing Beck, Gracie would dash up to him and lick his face! They would curl up together, and if I needed to leave for a few hours, Beck's owner kept the two dogs in his rig. Gracie never forgot Beck: when she encountered him a year later, in a location new to us both, she was all over him. They chased each other around a small farm, tearing through pastures and up and down the dirt road, leaping and lunging for joy.

I keep hoping we'll meet another such playmate for Gracie, but, so far, although she's often game to mingle, she still doesn't play. Our affable friend Beck ran off one day in January, 2014, bolting from his owner's truck during a travel stop at a Walmart near Okefenokee, Georgia. Without tags, despite many inquiries, he has not been found. His owner has since rescued another dog, but we will always miss Beck.

Beck is my best friend. Where are you, Beck?

See also **Toys** and **Tags**.

Poets

Forty years ago, when my son, Dylan Kuhn, turned ten, we went by train from California to New York to survey the Big Apple from the Twin Towers, climb the Statue of Liberty and see "Cats," the musical based on poems by T.S. Eliot. I have loved Eliot's cat poems since college, but I'd never read a book of poems devoted to dogs by a recognized poet until I discovered *Dog Songs,* by my favorite living poet, Mary Oliver, whom I once actually met. In her latest book, the long-time dog owner and rescuer celebrates her canine charges, present and departed.

"Ha!" I chortled to Gracie. "If a Pulitzer Prize winner can write about her dogs, I can write about you!"

Poop

Gracie is a superpooper. I have to warn friends who volunteer to walk her in my absence to take enough poopy bags. Perhaps only small dogs poop a lot—when I accompanied a friend walking her German shepherd, the big dog pooped only once.

Picking up dog poop is best approached with a positive spin. I try to think of my poop-scooping chore as a lower back exercise, like stooping for Ping Pong balls. I'm lucky that my back can cope. People who don't have dogs can't imagine why I would be willing to do this disgusting thing day after day, month after month, year after year, but, for me, that just makes it part of ordinary life.

I started recycling plastic grocery bags, which were prone to tearing—it took only one horrifying experience for me to learn to check poopy bags for holes. Looking for alternatives, I purchased a roll of 100 pick-up bags at a dollar store, but they, too, tore easily. During a trip to Vermont, at a bargain store, I bought a box of 210 Zippy Paws Pick-Up Bags. Made for pet waste disposal and at less than 4¢ each, these bags were strong, fit nicely in a jacket pocket and reduced the foul smell. I have become skilled at making one bag go for two poops. When I run out, I find many affordable biodegradable pick-up bag options online.

The firmness and color of Gracie's poops reflect her plumbing fitness. I worried about her loose stools when she first arrived, but, as I hoped, it was a just reaction to new surroundings. A neighbor I met at the dog park suggested I add some canned pumpkin to her food, but Gracie, who will eat almost anything, refused it. Eventually she fell into her two-to-four-poop-walk routine.

See also **Grass**.

Quarantine

When I recently turned down an invitation to spend a month in Paris, I had to become philosophical and remind myself that, although I can no longer travel on a whim, my present path has held new adventures and worthwhile rewards. During my forty years as a full-time writer and artist I have learned that I can have it all, just not all at once.

However, a Rick Steves radio program recently suggested that traveling to Paris with a pet may not be a pipe dream after all. With the required papers and immunization, I might be able to walk Gracie along the Seine without our having to endure a long quarantine.

The French really love their dogs. When I was in Paris years ago, I observed dogs sitting at restaurant tables. Sightseeing, I had to watch my step—poopy bags were not yet widely in use. (Members of a consciousness-raising group were sticking a little French flag in each pile.) At the moment, some airlines allow dogs under twenty pounds to travel in the cabin in a crate that fits under the seat. Today, if I were to plan a trip abroad with Gracie, I'd check the internet for the latest regulations, which appear to differ, country to country.

So far, however, our only experience of international travel has been taking a shortcut through Canada to visit my mother in Vermont. I checked regulations online for crossing the Canadian border and brought a passport for me and, for Gracie, proof of possession and current rabies immunization. My passport was checked by both Canadian and United States border officials, but they never requested Gracie's paperwork. Still, wherever I travel with my dog, I take her immunization records and health contacts, just in case.

Rain

Today, all-day rain has been forecast. We're camping, so we'll be cooped up all day in the RV. I watch the radar on my

My head still gets wet!

Mary's rain hat.

iPhone for an opportunity to pop out for a quick walk. I haven't figured out how to cover those perky ears, but, thanks to the plastic yellow raincoat I made from an upcycled Disney parka, most of Gracie will stay dry. I keep a towel by the van door to clean her muddy paws before she jumps on the bed.

Shedding

My mother, a careful housekeeper, used to despair at the sheer and endless volume of my brother's golden retriever's hair, so I hoped that, like a poodle or Siamese cat, Gracie wouldn't shed in my house. But the hair is there and it presents a serious challenge to my lint roller. Gracie's quarter-inch leavings are so hard to remove that I think of them as minutely armed, like porcupine quills or microscopically hooked grains of pollen. I take the considerable time required to pick clean my black cashmere sweater, but I have given away most of my other black clothing. My home's omnipresent layer of dog hair mostly goes unnoticed by my guests, unless they are allergic to it, or, heaven help us, they wear black.

Socialization (Hers)

Gracie's aggression toward other dogs has been our biggest challenge: nothing raises Gracie's hackles—the dark line of fur along her spine—like the sudden appearance of another dog. (Until Gracie, I didn't know what hackles were.) Most of our initial problems—bolting, barking, marking inside, not coming when called, obnoxious behavior toward guests and leash tugging—have been tolerably solved by training, equipment, treats and time, but Gracie still goes into a frenzy when we meet another dog on a trail, or see one across the street, and she almost chokes herself.

Biskit and Gypsy are my favorite farm friends.

Helping Gracie overcome her fear of other dogs was high on my to-do list. Soon after returning from our first Florida winter, I took Gracie to Kaybee's, the training and boarding facility recommended by my local dog-owner friends. The staff worked with Gracie until she could be corralled with other dogs and not always crated by herself. Every time I picked her up, I received a report card grading her various behaviors. Although our patronage may have been encouraged by positivity, her reports were never terrible, and Gracie did improve. She quickly learned what was unacceptable at Kaybees, and she never resisted entering. Some of those lessons even made it home.

We have made some progress. Gracie can safely run on the farm with dogs from cereal-bowl- to goat-size. She's stopped chasing the horses or barking at the ponies that, turned loose at night, snuffle around our van. She's well-behaved when she's boarded. But if she is on a leash and approached by an on-leash dog, Gracie still goes nuts. Often, I have to pick up her squirming body before we pass. I dread these encounters and I do what I can to avoid them. In town I've learned to change direction if I see an approaching dog walker, but on a trail or in a campground, the only way is through.

Usually she just wants to check out the approaching dog. If I allow her to go up to the dog (with its owner's permission), she will now often do the friendly butt-sniffing thing: Gracie has a fascination with other dogs' butts. Last summer we were visiting a friend on his father's dairy farm when a tail-wagging farm dog loped up and started sniffing Gracie's butt. "Oh that's gross!" said my friend. I was surprised, as he was a farmer himself, and even I knew that, when dogs circle nose to butt, they are just introducing themselves. However indelicate it may appear, I'm always relieved when Gracie sniffs a dog's butt instead of raising her hackles.

I've tried to encourage Gracie to trust other people by inviting friends to the house and taking her to visit them when I was sure she'd be welcome. She learned to get along at the dog park. Right from the start, though, Gracie surprised me by walking calmly through crowds gathered to enjoy our annual St. Patrick's Day Parade, or our summer art street fair. Away from home, with no territory to defend,

See how nice I am with this horse? I'm not even barking!

unless we encounter a dog, Gracie has been well behaved. Perhaps I can even take her to book signings!

Gracie doesn't like to be alone. I've been tempted at times to find her a companion, especially when I ignore her for hours to focus on, well, writing this book. When I mention this temptation to my dear friend, Mary—I'm sure I've brought it up more than once—she makes me promise that, before I do such a thing, I will call her. "Gracie does not need another dog," she assures me, and I'm sure she means that I don't need another dog. I'm lucky to have a friend like Mary, who sometimes knows my limits better than I do.

Socialization (Mine)

Having Gracie seems to have made me more approachable—perfect strangers often talk to me now, asking what kind of dog is that, or what's her name, or may they pet her. Gracie is a conversation starter, something a loner like me can use. I have even become friends with other dog owners, an acquaintance initiated purely because our dogs had sniffed butts.

I doubt I had ever enquired after anybody's cat, dog or parakeet, until one day I suddenly realized how much people like to be asked about their pets. I've also noticed how much I appreciate being asked about Gracie. "How's Gracie," a friend might ask. "How's that cute little dog of yours?" And off I go, yakking about my dog.

Recently, a friend I like, but don't know very well, came over to help me fold note cards. We had to make conversation for quite a long time. She was so nice to Gracie that I asked her if she had a dog. No, she didn't have a dog, although she used to have one, and I found out quite a lot about it, but not as much as I found out about her cat. She really enjoyed telling me about her cat, and I enjoyed hearing about it.

So now, if I am stumped for a conversation starter, I am going to ask if this person has a dog. Almost everyone has had a dog at one time or another, or, if not a dog, a cat, a ferret, or a parakeet. Since I don't have grandchildren, I'd rather hear about their pets, and I might even get a word in about Gracie.

So far no one has asked me about my childhood pets, which

is just as well, as I wasn't allowed any. Should someone ask, however, I might dig up an exception: when I was about nine, while our family lived in Murree, West Pakistan, my mission-ary doctor father purchased two wild, squat green parrots from some local boys. He made a cage for our new pets from pine limbs and chicken wire, which he hung up in a tree. Every morning our birds attracted a noisy flock of relatives, so we soon turned our parrots loose. I envied my best friend, Marty Vroon, whose family shared our mountain apartment complex, for her cute pet cocker spaniel.

These days, less social than I used to be, it's nice having a lively companion as I work at home, do errands, or travel. The house would seem awfully quiet without the bump of Gracie jumping off a bed, or jingling inside from the yard, toenails clicking on the hardwood floors. Sometimes, when I see some-one walking along our favorite stretch of rail trail alone, I think about the many years I walked, hiked, or jogged by myself, and how much nicer it feels now to walk with a dog.

Squirt Bottle

I use a squirt bottle—I notice it contains the word "quirt"—as a last resort. It stops short of physical violence, which I've long believed leads to more violence and the notion that might makes right. Fear-inspired obedience seems to me an unreli-able, no-fun path to desirable behavior.

Positive reenforcements, however, like treats, approval, praise, food, loyalty, love, increased freedom and natural consequences worked pretty well for me as the mother of a small child. Now, as then, I sometimes have to remind myself that punishment is often a shortcut to training I am tempted to skip or give short shrift. Patience in the short run has sometimes saved me years of misery.

On the dicey subject of discipline, I should confess that I have at times used isolation as punishment, as in "Go to your room!" It seemed a softer way to urge my child toward good behavior. Now that I am dealing with Gracie's basement-and-bathroom phobias, I'm wondering if isolation is actually just a passive aggressive form of violence—in some cultures, shunning serves as the ultimate punishment.

I digress. Anyway, the worst punishment I have used on Gracie is a squirt, or two, or three, from a water bottle—a useful suggestion from our soft-hearted trainer. "Really soak her," insisted Kristine. Thanks to Gracie's aversion to getting wet, the blast does get her attention. Oh, the hurt look I get from my dripping dog! However, improved manners have earned her more time outside to bask in the sun. Our walks are becoming friendlier. And although certain RV park neighbors still call her "Tasmaniac," progress is being made.

See also **Barking**.

Tags

On our second day together, I took Gracie to our county animal control agency to get her licensed. This required proof of her rabies inoculation and my adoption papers. We received a red metal numbered tag, which I attached to her collar along with a second metal tag purchased from a local pet store. This I had engraved on the spot with her name on one side and my phone number on the other. In less than two hours and for under $30.00, I had ensured my little dog's safety, bought myself peace of mind and added to our lives a happy jingle that tells me where Gracie has got to.

Twice during our first year I forgot to close the gate. Each time Gracie ran off, and, each time, in less than ten minutes, a neighbor called, thanks to Gracie's tag. On the flip side, Gracie's beloved pal, Beck, was without tags when he wandered off. Should I become especially worried about Gracie being stolen or lost, I could have a microchip (the size of a grain of rice and containing relevant contact information) implanted under her skin and registered with the National Pet Microchip Registration Database.

See also **Playing**.

Teeth

Unless she's been eating horse poop, or something mysterious and even more disgusting, Gracie does not have bad breath. So I wasn't worried about her teeth until our veterinarian began bringing up tooth-brushing at every appointment. "It's very important that you brush Gracie's teeth daily," he urges every time we see him. (I wonder if he brushes those of his own five dogs every day.) Despite this advice, our doggie toothpaste and toothbrush, purchased two years ago, remain mostly unused.

Thirty years ago, when I had two collies and four cats, brushing their teeth had not occurred to me.

The only times Gracie has growled at me are during my attempts to brush her teeth. Following the vet's suggestion, I started with a fingerful of peanut-butter-flavored toothpaste, but Gracie made it clear that no part of me was welcome in her mouth. When, during our next vet visit, I complained of the problem, it was suggested that I work from behind my dog, so I could hold her still. Right.

I am worried. Gracie is now six years old and the vet has warned that, at some future date, she may require a risky, expensive procedure to scrape tartar off her teeth. Meanwhile, I buy those expensive green tooth-cleaning treats touted as effective measures, but which I doubt are a substitute for the brush. I was somewhat reassured when another vet recently checked Gracie's teeth and declared them "fine."

Recently, the weather being conducive, I let Gracie ride along to my semi-annual dental cleaning, and I left her in the car. "Oh, bring her in!" invited my wonderful dentist. When I reclined in the dental chair, Gracie, after accepting the kind attentions of all the entirely female staff, jumped in my lap, and, for half an hour, calmly watched my dental hygienist work on my teeth! It may have helped that Sue and I, after fifteen years and thirty appointments, have become friends and are very comfortable with each other. But still, what a doggie!

Therapy Dog

I never thought my Gracie, rarely affectionate on demand, could serve as a soothing therapy dog, but I was wrong. Last summer, we visited an old friend whom Gracie had never met, and who was in a late stage of Alzheimer's disease. Gracie jumped into the big man's lap and stayed there, practically purring, while he held her gently for almost half an hour. "That's the first time I've seen him smile in months," said his wife with tears in her eyes. Perhaps Gracie would make a fine therapy dog after all—she's certainly works for me.

Thief!

I was preparing the whole Thanksgiving shebang—beautifully set table, turkey in the oven, stuffing almost ready—when I went to the back porch to help my brother and his wife bring in their contributions. I didn't think much of an unusual clinking sound in the dining room until I spied Gracie, legs splayed among the wine glasses, digging into her second dish of butter. Relieved that my family did not insist on a clean tablecloth, I picked up my little thief and wondered aloud if consuming more than a stick of butter in less than five minutes would make her seriously ill.

My M.D. brother Dewey suggested that, at ten times her weight, I'd have to eat ten sticks of butter—two-and-a-half pounds—to equal Gracie's feat. It was a holiday, an on-call vet only available for a minimum of $80. We decided to mash the potatoes, carve the turkey and keep an eye on her.

To my surprise, Gracie displayed no discomfort whatever, eagerly poised for the delicious aftermath of so many plates. It was only much later that night that she threw up on a quilt that twenty years ago had taken me most of a Beaver Island winter to complete. The next day the quilt went to the cleaners and the dog to the vet, who was concerned about pancreatitis, a serious condition I'd never heard of. But Gracie never did show any further symptoms.

This was not her only food fling. Eating lunch at my computer one day, I went to the kitchen to get some salsa for my green chili stew. I glanced out the window in time to witness a white tortilla vanishing into Gracie's jaws. Sure I'd had two, I dashed outside to rescue the second tortilla, lest, devouring that, too, she never pooped again. Too late. Only a ragged shred could I pull from those efficient jaws. Bad dog!

Later that same day, Gracie entered the house with the body of a house sparrow in her mouth. Where was its head? Had it joined the tortillas? Oh bad, bad dog!

That night Gracie was unusually affectionate, laying her head on my stomach as I watched a cooking show. Short memory, my eye—she knew. Oh yes, she did.

Toys

Gracie's passion for playthings came as quite a surprise to me. Gracie's not interested in the toys I think of when it comes to dogs—she won't chase balls or Frisbees—toys that don't

A toy is not a toy without a squeaky!

squeak don't interest her. But she loves retrieving a thrown stuffed squeaky toy. Requiring some attention after my hours at the computer, she might bring me one, or should I suggest, "Want to play?" she will race to her toy basket.

Fetch the Toy is played from the living room futon. Squeezing a loud SQUEAK! from, say, a monkey, I hurl it into the dining room, where it lands in a forest of chair legs. "GO GET YOUR TOY!" I cry.

Gracie leaps from the futon, scrambles across the room and returns in seconds, toy in jaws. She wants me to throw it again, but can't bring herself to release it. No amount of training has persuaded her to DROP IT! or GIVE IT TO ME! So I distract her by squeezing a second toy held behind my back. SQUEAK! Instantly, panting, ears on high alert, Gracie drops toy #1 and checks out the noise. I throw toy #2, and off she goes. We repeat the two-toy game until she gets wise to my ruse and retreats to a far corner to chew on her prize.

Noticing how pricey dog toys tend to be, I ordered a packet of plastic squeakies from eBay. I knot these into old socks and sew them into small stuffed animals I pick up at garage sales. Although Gracie is easy on her toys, often grooming them instead of chewing on them, from time to time, a repair becomes urgent. Gracie lies patiently nearby on the futon, her eyes glued to the big needle in my hand as I suture her lambie or monkey with embroidery or upholstery thread. She waits for the thrilling moment I return the toy to her jaws.

Okay! I chewed on Monkey a bit too hard! Now I have to watch Mary sew him up.

I always look for polyester fill in potential doggie toys—some children's stuffed toys are filled with little pellets a dog can choke on. I also snip off buttons, plastic eyes, or other embellishments that could be chewed off, just as I would on a toy intended for an infant.

Look what a great job she did!

Not all dogs are easy on soft toys—I've watched dogs turn a toy into a pile of stuffing in less than an hour. Gracie's toys, however, stick around. She chews only the treats and toys that I clearly give her, and even those she mostly just licks their fur. Her first and

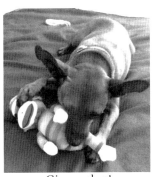

Gimme that!

favorite toy—a small version of Sheri Lewis's Lamb Chop, now more than two years old—has survived more surgeries that I have, but we're still here.

Lambie is still my favorite.

Treats

What a time I have had finding the right treats for a small dog. Of course, almost anything is a treat for Gracie, even nuggets of her own dry dog food; the challenge for me was not just the size, but the price: A chew-type treat, often demolished in minutes, may cost up to a dollar. Then there's the health threat that comes with some brands made abroad.

At first, I only found cat treats small enough for training, when I'd use a lot in a short time. I soon learned that cat treats are too high in protein for dogs and can cause kidney problems. Very sorry to hear that, I resumed the hunt. I noticed that my vet rewarded her charges' bravery with small soft treats, but the bags looked expensive.

At last I purchased a bag of Old Mother Hubbard P-Nuttier bone-shaped snacks at Tractor Supply, and I found Charlee Bear Dog Treats at the Trader Joe's. A friend suggested I look for kibble-sized treats in my supermarket's bulk food section. In the end, I bought so many treats to try, we're still working through them, breaking the too-biggies into usable pieces. When we finally run out, I'll bake up a batch from one of the many online dog treat recipes, using the bone-shaped cookie cutters we last year received as a gift.

Vacuum Cleaners and Lawn Mowers

Gracie cannot resist pouncing on the business end of the vacuum cleaner as it glides across the floor. The lawn mower and snow-blower are such predictable jaw magnets that, for her safety, Gracie is banished to the house when they are in use. Apparently, Gracie is not the only dog to launch surprise attacks on these ferocious appliances—friends confirm similar experiences with their dogs. Attempting to understand this odd behavior, I theorize that the loud moving machines are exhibiting alpha behavior smack in the middle Gracie's territory, and she simply will not have it.

Veterinarians

I take Gracie to an animal hospital where, so far, she has been seen by three veterinarians, all pleasant and helpful. The front desk people are friendly, and I can promptly get an appointment. Gracie now has two years of records there, including all her immunizations, and I like being reminded by e-mail when something is due. At each visit she is weighed, which helps me portion her meals.

Our vets understand how attached I am to Gracie, and they take my concerns seriously. I appreciate their gentle treatment of my little dog, who bravely tolerates their proddings and pokings. Gracie doesn't resist going to the vet, and, except for wait times rivaling my rheumatologist's, I don't either.

Having heard that veterinarians can vary widely in cost and quality of care, I consulted my local dog-owner friends, who were unanimous in their recommendations. I still shake my head every time I write a check.

Voice (Hers)

We may not understand what we are saying, but we always know who's saying it. At a recent library book and media sale, I spotted a black LP label which pictured a white dog and a large-horned gramophone. I thought, whoever came up with "My Master's Voice" must have had a dog. My dog knows my voice, even if she doesn't always respond to it. I also know hers. I can easily distinguish her bark from the other dogs' when we're travelling. At home, I can tell from inside if it's Gracie barking in the yard or the poodle across the fence.

Gracie has other ways to communicate. Some time during our second year, Gracie began making a humming sound deep in her throat. I worried that she was in pain but finally realized it was a pleasure groan—anticipation of a walk when I'm putting on my shoes, or relief at seeing me emerge from the shower. Sneezes may result from too much excitement, or frustration at my astonishing slowness to understand her. Lately, Gracie has permitted herself a little WOOF! It seems to mean, "Sorry to disturb you, Mary, but I need something." I get to guess what that is.

Voice (Mine)

I used to mock that British TV dog trainer, Barbara Woodhouse, for her oddly intoned WALKIES! Now I think she was on to something—Gracie seems most responsive to a high voice that I'd be embarrassed to use with people. "Come along," I sing-song to my little dog when she tugs on her leash, and, most of the time, she does. When I use this tone of voice, Gracie knows I am talking to her and not on the phone, or, having lived so long alone, to myself.

One day, after listening to a television ad for Beggin' Strips, I realized that I was hearing me. "There you go!" I carol as I pour Gracie's chow in her bowl. I often repeat what I say to Gracie, as if she were hard of hearing, even though her ears function better than mine.

I shunned baby talk when Dylan was born, but I have to confess to doggie talk. Despite being an English literature major, I now let the word "doggie" can leave my mouth. I can't seem to help myself, and I can't bring myself to describe it. I'm just careful not to be heard by anyone but Gracie.

Dogs, I've read, have poor memories, especially short-term. This seems true for Gracie, who can be easily distracted. On the other hand, without an active memory, how could she be trained? How can she trust in her safety, or anticipate her routine pleasures? Although I've taken care not to use it, I wonder if she'd respond to her old name, or to a voice from her past. If we were parted for years, would she remember mine?

Vomit

Since the Thanksgiving butter episode, the last time Gracie threw up, I later found a chewed-up squirrel carcass next to the garage. Another time, I could make out upchucked parts of a June bug. Vomit always worries me. So far, however, Gracie has quickly recovered with no evident loss of appetite.

So how are dogs able to eat rotten and filthy things that would surely send me to the emergency room? And how can Gracie eat off the kitchen floor with never a noticeable consequence, while any fork or spoon I happen to drop goes straight into the dishwasher? Researching these questions, I discovered that a dog's stomach is so large, muscular and unusually acidic, it can digest bones and turn ineffective many kinds of harmful bacteria. Conversely, dog's intestines and bowels are typically shorter than those in humans, hence the swift elimination of last night's dinner. (These amazing stomach capabilities may explain, at long last, Gracie's vanishing bone trick.)

Dogs also have a regurgitation instinct that lets them throw up improperly processed food and—sorry to say this—re-swallow it. I've seen Gracie do this. It seemed disgusting at the time, so I discouraged her from re-eating it, but perhaps I should have just let her be.

See also **Health (Hers)**.

Walking

I think Gracie would rather walk than eat. If I pick up a shoe, jacket, or set of keys, she is soon dancing around the house, darting between front door and back, lest I sneak out one or the other without her, and pausing only so I can clip on her leash. Although today our walks are mostly pleasant, they didn't start out that way.

Gracie was a yanker, fifteen pounds of muscle and dogged energy, and she looked like the little toughie she was in the

If Mary had had rollerskates, I could have given her quite a ride wearing this harness.

harness she came in. I thought a harness would be preferable for a dog that pulled. Not so—although a big dog may be more easily controlled with a harness, it enabled Gracie to haul me down the sidewalk. This endless yanking took the joy out of our walks and posed a serious threat to my rotator cuff injury. Something had to be done.

I began by replacing her collar with a Martindale collar—an inch-wide canvas strap with a plastic snap buckle. It held her tags and provided a loop that, when attached to a line or leash, tightened if she pulled. The Martindale collar ensured that Gracie didn't slip her narrow head out of her collar when she was on a line, but it didn't stop her from pulling or lunging after other dogs, even when it tightened around her neck.

I took up Gracie's habitual leash-yanking with Kristine Felke, our trainer, after we first returned from Florida. "Every time Gracie pulls on the leash, stop, turn around and walk her in the opposite direction," advised Kristine. If I'd repeat this half an hour a day, she assured me, Gracie would eventually stop pulling. The key word here is "eventually." The stop-and-turn method probably would have worked if I'd kept it up for a month with never a normal walk to be had, but Gracie outlasted me. Also aggravated by snowy sidewalks, I probably ran out of patience.

Sorry to hear about my lack of success with the stop-and-turn method, my veterinarian suggested I try the "Gentle Leader." Purchased for $25.00, this harness was so complicated that it came with a DVD. I finally figured out how to get it on her—it fit over the muzzle (such a funny word, like nuzzle)—but our test walk was not encouraging. When Gracie pulled, her head was forced to one side. This did slow her down, but constantly looking sideways made forward progress awkward. Nor did she appreciate her jaws being strapped shut.

As I woman, often charged with the welfare of others, I learned long ago that if I don't take care of myself, I can't take care of anyone else. "Me first," isn't an alpha thing; it's a gift to myself and the people I love. Gracie's aggression was aggravating the tendonitis in my wrists and threatening to reinjure my shoulder. So, after all efforts to stop her leash-pulling had failed, I bought a pinch collar from a nearby pet supply store, which offered several sizes.

I don't really mind the pinch collar. When Mary picks it up, I know it's walk time!

Try not to let a pinch collar get tangled!

A pinch collar consists of curved, metal, medieval-looking prongs hooked together in a circle—I could adjust its circumference to fit Gracie by adding, or removing, links. The pinch collar has proved so effective that we still use it. I attach it to Gracie's leash and slip it over her head, prongs out, so they don't poke her in the eye, turning the prongs in only when I anticipate a problem. People often glare at me when they see it. "That's a pretty serious collar for a little dog," some say. "She's a serious dog," I reply.

I'm always grateful to the rare observer who nods knowingly and smiles.

We did our final training session with one of Kirstine's assistants, who disapproved of the pinch collar that I'd found so effective. She brought us a harness ($21.95) to use instead. Gracie stood quietly while I struggled with a plastic clip that fastened under her chest—I would have had to lay on my back like an auto mechanic to see what I was doing. The next day, the new harness worked just great—Gracie did not tug—until she dashed after a squirrel, hit the end of the line and was flipped

Yikes! I did a double-flip in this harness!

into a somersault! Yikes! Minutes later, it happened again. Fortunately, Gracie escaped injury, and the harness was returned.

Gracie's never shown any sign of discomfort from her pinch collar and my vet assures me that she is not harmed. It's turned our daily walk into a much anticipated pleasure. When not in use, the pinch collar sometimes gets so hooked on itself that it feels like a Chinese puzzle. The first time that happened, I almost tossed it out to buy another. Eventually, I took the links apart and reassembled them. Now I somehow manage to disentangle it in a minute or two.

Down a thousand sidewalks, and, thanks to the pinch collar, Gracie didn't pull much any more, but she'd still goes nuts—and I'd yell—every time we'd see an approaching dog. I hate yelling at my dog, and, no matter how loudly I yelled, nothing ever changed. Finally, remembering that "Crazy is doing the same thing over and over and expecting different results," I began to practice Kirstine's stop-and-turn tactic—silently and firmly, I'd haul my dog in the opposite direction. Did that fix the problem? It hasn't fixed Gracie, but it did fix me—I don't have to listen to myself yelling at my dog.

One day, as we walked through a park toward the Saginaw River, I observed a family already there, playing with three large, off-leash dogs. I stopped in my tracks, wondering how to proceed.

"You need one of these," said a voice behind me. An older couple, a small dog in the woman's arms—no doubt, protecting it from Gracie—approached us. The man held out a small white spray can labelled HALT! "Just pointing the can is usually enough," he said. "People quickly call their dogs, begging you not to use it. It won't injure a dog, but its eyes will sting for a little while."

Not finding the pepper spray repellent in town, I easily purchased it online. Although I've never used it, I carry it in a fanny pack, especially when walking in Florida, where the big black vultures often hunt in packs and are rumored to take small dogs and peck their eyes out. Horrified by such a possibility, when the vultures circle in, as they sometimes do when we're walking, I swing the heavy carabiner at the end of Gracie's leash and wave my can of Halt!

Averaging about a mile a day, Gracie and I walk at least three-hundred-and-sixty miles a year, totaling, so far, over eight-hundred. Imagine! I try to vary our walks, exploring new blocks in town or trails in the woods. We've encountered buzzards, pelicans, dolphins, snakes, deer, ponies, cows, goats, dogs of all shapes and sizes and thousands of migrating birds. I've trod in boots, sneakers and sandals, and Gracie has pooped on grass, leaves, weeds and snow. We avoid farm roads, however tempting and plentiful a venue—farm dogs often run free and are often protective of their territory.

Our walking has other restraints: My old "dogs" will cover only so much ground, and, even though I carry a water bottle and we take breaks, the heat soon gets Gracie panting. So we will not be further impressing ourselves with our mileage. No matter—Gracie gets us out of the house.

See also **Leashes**.

Winter

I'm not into winter sports, so, for me, December brings shoveling and cabin fever, not downhill thrills. Gracie hates winter. She puts off setting a paw in snow until she reaches an urgency that is hard for me to recognize unless she is standing at the door. Soon her paw pockets fill with BBs of ice, and she is limping.

Gracie's legs can't clear anything higher than four inches. If the snow is deep, I shovel a path through the back yard so she won't sink out of sight. My attendance is required for winter rescues as, all four paws filled with ice balls, Gracie may find herself frozen in more ways than one. I plod through the drifts in my Uggs, pick her up, clean her paws with freezing bare fingers, and, if her mission has not yet been accomplished, release her to try again.

Booties have been suggested, but I doubt they'd stay on. She'd have no

Enough white stuff! Let's go to Florida!

110

grip and might soon be splayed on the icy driveway. Recently, my brother Dewey suggested that I spread the bottoms of her feet with Musher's Secret, a wax and lanolin concoction made for sled dogs and available online. I've ordered a jar, but we are far from next winter and unable to test the stuff.

We don't walk much when ice slicks the sidewalks. The last time I strapped on crampons—sharp metal cleats—to keep me vertical, one came off in a snowbank; I didn't find it until spring. So after a few weeks, when holiday jolliness and glistening landscapes have lost their charms, I begin the many trips between the RV and the house, packing a two-month supply of food staples, clothing, art supplies, reading material, gear and, of course, dog paraphernalia—food, coats, leash, lines, toys, meds, papers—the sheer amount of which reminds me of camping with a baby forty years ago.

The van stuffed to the gills, I study weather web sites for a no-snow route to Florida, plot a course, and drive the RV south, wondering what I'd forgotten this time. Once safely camped in warmer climes, I write and paint under the palms while Gracie sprawls in the sun. We tuck many a mild

Is that a
Tyrannasaurus Rex?

Now you're talking!

walking mile into our annual average. Every year, when winter threatens Michigan, I fantasize about this glorious option so often that, on arrival, I never fail to be re-amazed that it was not just a dream.

See also **Adventure**.

eXit

Whether our similarities first attracted us or we just have gotten that way, Gracie and I seem oddly alike. We strive to balance comfort and security with adventure and discovery. We both like people, parties and new places, but we tend to make our appearances brief. By the time I am ready to leave a place, Gracie is standing at the door. We are early exit-ers, not one of our more endearing behaviors. We thank our friends who forgive us and ask us back.

Of course, there's that final exit we don't dwell on: since she is now six, Gracie may keep me company until I am eighty.

If I take after my mother, Ruth Blocksma, presently a lively ninety-five, I am more likely to lose Gracie than she me. It's not something I like to think about, so I don't. Losing a dog is heart-breaking in a way that is hard for people who have never owned a dog to understand. Otherwise, I could only part with Gracie under terrible duress, like a medical catastrophe. Really, I can't bear to think of it.

Yawning

Gracie yawns so much that, at first, I wondered if she was getting enough sleep. When I Googled that behavior, I learned that dogs often yawn to release stress or excitement. That may explain Gracie's yawns, which now seem to signal that she's not getting what she wants when she wants it. She is showing frustration at my slowness, either getting the message or attending to it. Gracie's frequent yawns are silent, but so wide that I can observe that the top of the inside of her otherwise pink mouth is black. I always know I am misreading Gracie's clues when, once again, her jaws stretch wide, and she yawns.

Zee End

It was no secret that, except for a few beloved dogs belonging to friends, I never used to like dogs much. Dog owners at parties, indulging in endless doggie anecdotes, could talk me right out the door. Now, however, I too can go on and on. I am newly enjoying my dog-owner friends and our guiltless dog talk. Even more surprising, at least to myself, is how much I've come like most of the dogs I encounter. In just two years I've become a dog person. Dog people understand the deep connections that can grow between us and our canine companions. While I recognize that Gracie is a dog, she will never be just a dog.

A long-absent friend I saw again recently commented that I was looking more relaxed than usual, and I realized that I was finding my early seventies surprisingly contented. I adopted Gracie as I was turning seventy-one, so she probably has had something to do with it.

An acquaintance once confided that she never reads dog books because she always cries at the end. Well, this one doesn't have a sad ending. Gracie and I are flourishing, at home and on the road. We keep learning about one another, adventuring and meeting new friends. Although adopting Gracie felt crazy at first, taking care of her has become as ordinary as taking care of myself. Now that I think about it, caring for Gracie IS taking care of myself.

Just call me Chessie.

Acknowledgements

How could I ever have finished this book without my family and my Michigan friends who listened to my Gracie stories even when they didn't have a dog? To the many dog owners who offered advice when I really needed it—especially Brenda and Allan Brouillet, Marie Marfia, and Ann Yandell—I cheerfully thank you. I'm grateful to Pam and Jim Johnson, for their crucial guidance and the run of their of Ocala, Florida, horse farm; and to our trainer, Kristine Felske of Kaybees K-9 Training & Spa in Bay City, Michigan, for her expertise. For an editing job beyond my wildest dreams, I thank Pam Johnson; and for early readings, long-time dog-rescuer Murry deSanto and another kind heart, Shawna Davidson Guist, of Amazing Grace Animal Rescue in Saginaw.

I am grateful to my book club for unfailing enthusiasm, to Mary Briggs Bush for weekly cheering me on; to Jenny Blair for her charming drawing on page 47; to my brother, Dewey Blocksma, for his excellent feedback; to Dennis Malone for taking my picture in Florida with my iPhone; and to Martin M. Sielinski for his helpful art and photograph suggestions.

To all those at Sunset Isle RV Park in Cedar Key, Florida, who have endured our steep learning curve, our thanks for your patience and kindness. And cheers to Gracie, without whom there would be no book. I alone am responsible for the information, stories and errors in this book. To all of those I surely forgot to include here, please forgive me.

Look out! Here we come!